D1553220

15 DAYS OF PRAYER

WITH

Saint Alphonsus Liguori

JEAN-MARIE SÉGALEN, C.Ss.R.

Translated by Victoria Hébert and Denis Sabourin

Liguori

LIGUORI, MISSOURI

Published by Liguori Publications
Liguori, Missouri
www.liguori.org
www.catholicbooksonline.com

This book is a translation of *Prier 15 Jours Avec Saint Alphonse de Liguori*, published by Nouvelle Cité, 1995, Montrouge, France.

English Translation Copyright 2001 by Liguori Publications.

All rights reserved. No part of this publication may be reproduced, stored in a retrieval system, or transmitted in any form or by any means—electronic, mechanical, photocopy, recording, or any other—except for brief quotations in printed reviews, without the prior permission of the publishers.

Library of Congress Cataloging-in-Publication Data

Ségalen, Jean-Marie.
    [Prier 15 jours avec Saint Alphonse de Liguori. English]
    15 days of prayer with Saint Alphonsus Liguori / Jean-Marie Ségalen; translated by Victoria Hébert and Denis Sabourin. — 1st English ed.
        p. cm.
    Includes bibliographical references.
    ISBN 0-7648-0714-5 (pbk.)
    1. Liguori, Alfonso Maria de', Saint, 1696–1787—Meditations. 2. Spiritual life—Catholic Church. I. Title: Fifteen days of prayer with Saint Alphonsus Liguori. II. Title.

BX4700.L6 S4413 2001
269'.6—dc21   00-054955

Scripture quotations are taken from the *New Revised Standard Version Bible*, copyright 1989 by the Division of Christian Education of the National Council of the Churches of Christ in the U.S.A. Used by permission. All rights reserved.

Printed in the United States of America
05 04 03 02 01   5 4 3 2 1
First English Edition 2001

Table of Contents

How to Use This Book

AN OLD CHINESE PROVERB, or at least what I am able to recall of what is supposed to be an old Chinese proverb, goes something like this: "Even a journey of a thousand miles begins with a single step." When you think about it, the truth of the proverb is obvious. It is impossible to begin any project, let alone a journey, without taking the first step. I think it might also be true, although I cannot recall if another Chinese proverb says it, "that the first step is often the hardest." Or, as someone else once observed, "the distance between a thought and the corresponding action needed to implement the idea takes the most energy." I don't know who shared that perception with me but I am certain it was not an old Chinese master!

With this ancient proverbial wisdom, and the not-so-ancient wisdom of an unknown contemporary sage still fresh, we move from proverbs to presumptions. How do these relate to the task before us?

I am presuming that if you are reading this introduction it is because you are contemplating a journey. My presumption is that you are preparing for a spiritual journey and that you have taken at least some of the first steps necessary to prepare for this journey. I also presume, and please excuse me if I am making too many presumptions, that in your preparation for the spiritual journey you have determined that you need a guide. From deep within the recesses of your deepest self, there was something that called you to consider Saint Alphonsus as a potential companion. If my presumptions are correct, may I congratulate you on this decision? I think you have made a wise choice, a choice that can be confirmed by yet another source of wisdom, the wisdom that comes from practical experience.

Even an informal poll of experienced travelers will reveal a common opinion; it is very difficult to travel alone. Some might observe that it is even foolish. Still others may be even stronger in their opinion and go so far as to insist that it is necessary to have a guide, especially when you are traveling into uncharted waters and into territory that you have not yet experienced. I am of the personal opinion that a traveling companion is welcome under all circumstances. The thought of traveling alone, to some exciting destination without someone to share the journey with does not capture my imagination or channel my enthusiasm. However, with that being noted, what is simply a matter of preference on the normal journey becomes a matter of necessity when a person embarks on a spiritual journey.

The spiritual journey, which can be the most challenging of all journeys, is experienced best with a guide, a companion, or at the very least, a friend in whom you have placed your trust. This observation is not a preference or an opinion but rather an established spiritual necessity. All of the great saints with whom I am familiar had a spiritual director or a confessor who journeyed with them. Admittedly, at times the saint might well have traveled far beyond the experience of their guide and companion but more often than not they would return to their director and reflect on their experience. Understood in this sense, the director and companion provided a valuable contribution and necessary resource.

When I was learning how to pray (a necessity for anyone who desires to be a full-time and public "religious person"), the community of men that I belong to gave me a great gift. Between my second and third year in college, I was given a one-year sabbatical, with all expenses paid and all of my personal needs met. This period of time was called novitiate. I was officially designated as a novice, a beginner in the spiritual journey, and I was assigned a "master," a person who was willing to lead me. In addition to the master, I was provided with every imaginable book and any other resource that I could possibly need. Even with all that I was provided, I did not learn how to pray because of the books and the unlimited resources, rather it was the master, the companion who was the key to the experience.

One day, after about three months of reading, of quiet and solitude, and of practicing all of the methods and descriptions of prayer that were available to me, the master called. "Put away the books, forget the method, and just listen." We went into a room, became quiet, and tried to recall the presence of God, and then, the master simply prayed out loud and permitted me to listen to his prayer. As he prayed, he revealed his hopes, his dreams, his struggles, his successes, and most of all, his relationship with God. I discovered as I listened that his prayer was deeply intimate but most of all it was self-revealing. As I learned about him, I was led through his life experience to the place where God dwells. At that moment I was able to understand a little bit about what I was supposed to do if I really wanted to pray.

The dynamic of what happened when the master called, invited me to listen, and then revealed his innermost self to me as he communicated with God in prayer, was important. It wasn't so much that the master was trying to reveal to me what needed to be said; he was not inviting me to pray with the same words that he used, but rather that he was trying to bring me to that place within myself where prayer becomes possible. That place, a place of intimacy and of self-awareness, was a necessary stop on the journey and it was a place that I needed to be led to. I could not have easily discovered it on my own.

The purpose of the volume that you hold in your hand is to lead you, over a period of fifteen days or, maybe more realistically, fifteen prayer periods, to a place where prayer is possible. If you already have a regular experience and practice of prayer, perhaps this volume can help lead you to a deeper place, a more intimate relationship with the Lord.

It is important to note that the purpose of this book is not to lead you to a better relationship with Saint Alphonsus, your spiritual companion. Although your companion will invite you to share some of their deepest and most intimate thoughts, your companion is doing so only to bring you to that place where God dwells. After all, the true measurement of a companion for the journey is that they bring you to the place where you need to be, and then they step back, out of the picture. A guide who brings you to the desired destination and then sticks around is a very unwelcome guest!

Many times I have found myself attracted to a particular idea or method for accomplishing a task, only to discover that what seemed to be inviting and helpful possessed too many details. All of my energy went to the mastery of the details and I soon lost my enthusiasm. In each instance, the book that seemed so promising ended up on my bookshelf, gathering dust. I can assure you, it is not our intention that this book end up in your bookcase, filled with promise, but unable to deliver.

There are three simple rules that need to be followed in order to use this book with a measure of satisfaction.

Place: It is important that you choose a place for reading that provides the necessary atmosphere for reflection and that does not allow for too many distractions. Whatever place you choose needs to be comfortable, have the necessary lighting, and, finally, have a sense of "welcoming" about it. You need to be able to look forward to the experience of the journey. Don't travel steerage if you know you will be more comfortable in first class and if the choice is realistic for you. On the other hand, if first class is a distraction and you feel more comfortable and more yourself in steerage, then it is in steerage that you belong.

My favorite place is an overstuffed and comfortable chair in my bedroom. There is a light over my shoulder, and the chair reclines if I feel a need to recline. Once in a while, I get lucky and the sun comes through my window and bathes the entire room in light. I have other options and other places that are available to me but this is the place that I prefer.

Time: Choose a time during the day when you are most alert and when you are most receptive to reflection, meditation, and prayer.

The time that you choose is an essential component. If you are a morning person, for example, you should choose a time that is in the morning. If you are more alert in the afternoon, choose an afternoon time slot; and if evening is your preference, then by all means choose the evening. Try to avoid "peak" periods in your daily routine when you know that you might be disturbed. The time that you choose needs to be your time and needs to work for you.

It is also important that you choose how much time you will spend with your companion each day. For some it will be possible to set aside enough time in order to read and reflect on all the material that is offered for a given day. For others, it might not be possible to devote one time to the suggested material for the day, so the prayer period may need to be extended for two, three, or even more sessions. It is not important how long it takes you; it is only important that it works for you and that you remain committed to that which is possible.

For myself I have found that fifteen minutes in the early morning, while I am still in my robe and pajamas and before my morning coffee, and even before I prepare myself for the day, is the best time. No one expects to see me or to interact with me because I have not yet "announced" the fact that I am awake or even on the move. However, once someone hears me in the bathroom, then my window of opportunity is gone. It is therefore important to me that I use the time that I have identified when it is available to me.

Freedom: It may seem strange to suggest that freedom is the third necessary ingredient, but I have discovered that it is most important. By freedom I understand a certain "stance toward life," a "permission to be myself and to be gentle and understanding of who I am." I am constantly amazed at how the human person so easily sets himself or herself up for disappointment and perceived failure. We so easily make judgments about ourselves and our actions and our choices, and very often those judgments are negative, and not at all helpful.

For instance, what does it really matter if I have chosen a

place and a time, and I have missed both the place and the time for three days in a row? What does it matter if I have chosen, in that twilight time before I am completely awake and still a little sleepy, to roll over and to sleep for fifteen minutes more? Does it mean that I am not serious about the journey, that I really don't want to pray, that I am just fooling myself when I say that my prayer time is important to me? Perhaps, but I prefer to believe that it simply means that I am tired and I just wanted a little more sleep. It doesn't mean anything more than that. However, if I make it mean more than that, then I can become discouraged, frustrated, and put myself into a state where I might more easily give up. "What's the use? I might as well forget all about it."

The same sense of freedom applies to the reading and the praying of this text. If I do not find the introduction to each day helpful, I don't need to read it. If I find the questions for reflection at the end of the appointed day repetitive, then I should choose to close the book and go my own way. Even if I discover that the reflection offered for the day is not the one that I prefer and that the one for the next day seems more inviting, then by all means, go on to the one for the next day.

That's it! If you apply these simple rules to your journey you should receive the maximum benefit and you will soon find yourself at your destination. But be prepared to be surprised. If you have never been on a spiritual journey you should know that the "travel brochures" and the other descriptions that you might have heard are nothing compared to the real thing. There is so much more than you can imagine.

A final prayer of blessing suggests itself:

> Lord, catch me off guard today.
> Surprise me with some moment of beauty
>   or pain
> So that at least for the moment
> I may be startled into seeing that you are
>   here in all your splendor,
> Always and everywhere,
> Barely hidden,
> Beneath,
> Beyond,
> Within this life I breathe.

Frederick Buechner

REV. THOMAS M. SANTA, CSsR
LIGUORI, MISSOURI
FEAST OF THE PRESENTATION, 1999

Introduction and Chronology

WHO IS SAINT ALPHONSUS LIGUORI?

A few years ago, more precisely, in 1977, when Father Théodule Rey-Mermet was preparing his book, *Saint Alphonsus Liguori: Tireless Worker for the Most Abandoned*, I was going with him to visit some "Alphonsian" sites that were mentioned in his work. Surprisingly, our car broke down just as we were approaching Naples. It was already noon by the time we got off the highway, stopped at Capoue, and found a mechanic to fix the car. On the other side of the street, there was an inn which was deserted at that hour. We entered and ordered a plate of spaghetti. The innkeeper, intrigued by the presence of two strangers, approached us and asked, "Where are you from? Where are you going? What are you doing?" Father Rey-Mermet replied that we had come from France to study documents concerning the history of Saint Alphonsus Liguori. He added: "You are from Naples, you must know who Saint Alphonsus Liguori is." There was silence! Suddenly, the innkeeper, who probably had just vague memories of the catechism and the sermons of his parish priest, cried out, as if he was given a sudden illumination: "Oh yes, he was one of the Twelve!" Surprise! We looked at him with a smile. In this reply, which seemed to be somewhat comical, there was a great deal of truth. In effect, even though Saint Alphonsus was not one of the Twelve Apostles, was he not a missionary just as they were?

THE MOST SAINTLY OF THE NEAPOLITANS,
THE MOST NEAPOLITAN OF THE SAINTS

Then who was Saint Alphonsus? Alphonsus Maria Liguori (Alfonso Maria di Liguori) was born at Marianella (*Marianelli* in Italian), about five miles from Naples, Italy, on September 27, 1696, to a well-established family of the nobility.

When we took our trip to Naples in 1977, we went on a pilgrimage to visit the Santa-Maria-dei-Vergini Church, where he had been baptized. The bombs of the Second World War had spared the baptistery, and when we came to the sacristy, we consulted the baptismal registry for the year 1696. We opened it to page 127. There, we could just make out, in the margins around the actual act of Alphonsus's baptism, the following notations in various different styles of handwriting: "beatified in September, 1816"; "canonized on May 26, 1839"; and "declared a Doctor of the Church on March 23, 1871." On that occasion, Pope Pius IX stated: "He dissipated the shadows of error spread by the disbelievers and Jansenists. Through wise works, especially through the learned treatises of his moral theology, he enlightened the obscure points and resolved all doubts. In the thicket of opinions of the theologians which were either too broad or too rigid, he cleared a safe path by which the directors of souls could walk with a step that was free from entanglements." Later, on April 26, 1950, Pius XII declared Alphonsus to be "the patron of all moralists and confessors."

Holding a doctorate in both civil and ecclesiastical law, and a lawyer, Alphonsus left the bar in order to become a priest. Ordained at the age of thirty, he dedicated himself to an apostolate with the downtrodden and, in 1732, founded a congregation that was devoted to the evangelization of the "most abandoned souls of the rural areas": the Congregation of the Most Holy Redeemer (CSsR, the Redemptorists). In 1762, Pope Clement XIII forced him to accept the responsibilities of being a bishop. At the age of seventy-nine, due to his infirmities, he was relieved of his responsibilities and returned to his congregation. He left us with a plethora of written works—111 in all. He died on August 1, 1787.

Jean Delumeau, of the College of France, wrote the following about him: "Saint Alphonsus was a giant, a giant in the history of spirituality and of recent history...the numbers are all there...by the number of books, Saint Alphonsus clearly and decidedly beats out Shakespeare: his first, by about 20,000 editions in more than 70 languages, his second by 10,602 editions (as of 1961), in 77 languages" (SSL, p. 7).

That was a saint! A great saint! But he was a saint who suffered a great deal at the hands of his biographers. How many legends there are circulating about him! They continue to circulate even today, in works that do nothing but reproduce errors about him because of a lack of serious documentation, and because they have not read Théodule Rey-Mermet's book, *Saint Alphonsus Liguori: Tireless Worker for the Most Abandoned*. This is the most complete biography of Alphonsus Liguori, a work that was awarded the 1987 History Prize from the French Academy. This remarkable book brings about a much needed "tuning up" of his history, and served as an inspiration for this present little book.

Thus, we have described Alphonsus as an "anguished man," devoured by scruples, yet he was a man who was undeniably balanced, conscious of his responsibilities and possessed with rigorous integrity, even if he experienced, at the end of his life, psychological problems associated with his advanced age.

We have described him as a "distracted lawyer" who would lose a great international case because of a small oversight, yet he was a professional whose competence, at the age of twenty-seven, was recognized in the courts of Europe, who lost none of his cases save the very last, essentially because of the dishonesty of his adversaries.

We have described him as a founder who "was chased away from the congregation" he had founded, yet he was always loved by his brothers, but a victim of the hostility that pitted the king of Naples against the pontiff in Rome. He was not really "chased" from his institute in that sense of the word, but it had been cut in two by a papal decision: in 1780, in effect, Pius VI refused to recognize the houses located in the kingdom of Naples. Until his death, Alphonsus suffered because of this separation, always proclaiming that it would soon be reunified. And later, the pope publicly regretted having "tortured a saint." As for Alphonsus, he also complained of having been chased from his institute which was with respect to his elevation to the episcopate (office of bishop).... This event made him say, in the presence of his colleagues, on March 19, 1762: "God is chasing me from the congregation because of my sins...remember that..." (SSL, p. 476).

A TIRELESS WORKER FOR THE MOST ABANDONED, AND A SAINT FOR TODAY

He was a providential saint. In the eighteenth century, Saint Alphonsus pulled the Church away from fear and Jansenism. He opened it to hope but, above all, through his writings, he worked for the penetration of Christian spirituality into all walks of life, including even the poorest. Daniel Rops called him "the Vincent de Paul of the eighteenth century." He was, in effect, the man for the poor, the man for missions. But he went to the poor in the Church, with the missionary community he founded: he "staked his tent" in the midst of the people who had been abandoned by the pastoral work of the times. He revealed the Good News of salvation and the love of God to them. He taught them to believe and how to pray so they could convert and become true children of God by letting them edify themselves in the Holy Spirit, through the risen Jesus. His doctrine, as Daniel Rops stresses, "was characterized by a wisdom and a sense of equity that make him the most useful Christian thinker of the era, and also through him, the path to the future is opened.... Today, two centuries later, when we consider Saint Alphonsus Liguori's doctrine, we can only conclude that it contained all of the great tenets of Catholicism.... There are very few elements of religious life that had been practiced in the nineteenth century whose roots we could not have traced back to this doctrine.... This wise and moderate man who, nevertheless, was such a vigorous fighter for

Christ...understood that the essential task was to pit the enemy philosophies against a living religion which was lived to the very depths of the being. And alone, in an era where the ecclesiology (theology as applied to the nature and structure of the Christian Church) appeared so deficient...he had the premonition that, in order to give the Church its full strength, it was not enough to just defend it in its capacity as an institution, but one must feed it with the true sources of life, to reconstitute it into 'the Mystical Body of Christ.' Much more than the ordinary, the Catholic soul of the new times would be one of 'Alphonsian' spirituality" (*The Church of the Classical Era, the Era of the Great Schisms*, Fayard, 1958, p. 407–8).

More recently, Pope John Paul II, in his letter, *Spiritus Domini*, of August 1, 1987, wrote:

> From the testimony of the history of the Church and the documents of popular piety, the writings of Saint Alphonsus always remain current....
>
> Saint Alphonsus was "a good friend of the people," of the little people, of the people from the poorest areas of Naples, then the capital of this kingdom, of the humble people, the artists and, above all, the people of the countryside. This sense of people characterizes the entire life of Alphonsus as he was a missionary, a bishop, a founder, and a writer.
>
> As "a missionary," he went in search of "the most ignorant and abandoned souls in the countryside and rural hamlets," addressing himself to them in the most appropriate and vivid manner. He renewed the preaching of the Word of God using his own methods and contents so that it would be simpler but exhilarating. He did it this way so that everyone could understand.
>
> This "founder" of a congregation wanted to have a group of disciples who, following his example, could make the radical choice in favor of the most abandoned and who would move to be close to them. As a "bishop," if

his house was open to all, the humble and poor were preferred. And, in their favor, he also promoted social and economic initiatives.

Finally, as a writer, Alphonsus always and singularly aimed to "respond to the needs of the Christian people." Almost all of his works, including his moral ones, were inspired by the people.... The popularity of our saint, which always carried him further, rests on his succinctness, his clarity, his simplicity, his optimism, and his graciousness which, at times, went as far as tenderness. At the root of his love of the people, there is the anguish of eternal salvation: to save oneself is to save others. And he not only ardently desired salvation, but also perfection, all the way to holiness. That is why his pastoral actions excluded no one: he wrote to and for everyone. Thus, he urged the pastors of the people of God, above all the bishops, priests, and religious to spare nothing in order to respond to the needs of the people.... He had a very high degree of the sense of the Church, a criteria that always accompanied his theological research and his pastoral practices, to the point that he, himself, became the voice of the Church (*Catholic Documentation*, no. 1947, p. 885).

On the occasion of the third centenary celebration of the birth of Saint Alphonsus Liguori (1696–1996), with the third millennium of the Christian era foreseen on the horizon, as the pope urged the entire Church to participate in a new evangelization of our world, it was (and still is today) good to welcome the message of this great saint as a gift from God. In effect, as Father Pierre Gérard, SJ, wrote: "Many of his institutions, choices, initiatives, and methods are amazingly still modern and could continue to inspire Christians today. In an era of 'renewal,' from the renewal of prayer to the renewal of missions, from conciliatory renewal to 'the preferential choice for the poor,' from the commitment of the lay people to the modern methods of social communication in service of the

Gospel, there is no domain in which we don't find ourselves on the paths opened by Alphonsus Liguori in his time" (Missi, no. 494, *Alphonsus Liguori, the Man of Renewal*).

In his book, *Saint Alphonsus Liguori: Tireless Worker for the Most Abandoned*, Father Théodule Rey-Mermet well summed up, in a few words, the exceptional status of this great saint: "There was one European Christian Century of Enlightenment which began between 1660–1680. Alphonsus was a great figure in it and more than that, he kept deep roots in the tradition and brought clarity and warmth, not only just to the few elite, but to the popular masses of the universal Church" (SSL, p. 11).

In fact, instead of considering reason to be a threat, Alphonsus optimistically put it to work for mankind and the believer. That is why, when faced with pastoral teachings that were ravaged by Jansenism and austerity, he fought methodically, tenaciously, and enthusiastically for a morality of conscience and freedom. That is why, when faced with routine devotions without meaning, he proposed a spirituality according to the colors of the Gospel in the language of the common people of his era. His works of piety bring the most humble people to the summits of holiness; because, in their hearts, his spirituality dissipates the shadows of fear and makes shine the faith in the mercy of God, the love of Christ in his passion, and the hope in Mary, the mother of Jesus and our Mother.

Lord, help me:
make me eternally yours
before I reach death.
Give me your love,
but an ardent love;
a strong love that makes me able
to vanquish all difficulties;
a perpetual love
that connects me to you without return.

O my beloved Redeemer, I love you,
and I hope for everything through the blood
you shed for me.
I also hope for everything through your intercession,
O Mary, my refuge, my hope and my mother.[1]

---

1. Saint Alphonsus Liguori is called the Doctor of Prayer. He prayed well and a great deal, he preached a great deal about prayer as well as writing about it. And he had the habit of ending each chapter of his books about spirituality with a prayer. That is the reason why each of the following fifteen days will end with an extract from one of his numerous prayers. (Prayer above taken from *Religious State*, volume II in the collection *Spiritual Works of Saint Alphonsus*, p. 260.)

Abbreviations Used in This Book

The following is a list of references for the majority of the texts cited in this book. The titles of the books which have been translated into English are given with the original French titles in parentheses. If no English translation is available, only the French title is given. Further reading material is given at the end of the book.

AA   Saint Alphonsus Liguori, *The Practice of the Love of Jesus Christ*, Liguori Publications, Liguori, MO, 1997 (*L'Art d'Aimer Jesus Christ*)

GM   Saint Alphonsus Liguori, *The Glories of Mary*, complete in one volume, Liguori Publications, Liguori, MO, 2000 (*Les Gloires de Marie*)

N   Saint Alphonsus Liguori, *Meditations on the Incarnation* (*Noël*, Éd. Saint Paul)

VS   Saint Alphonsus Liguori, *The Way of Salvation* (*La Voie du Salut*, Éd. Saint Paul)

VSS   Saint Alphonsus Liguori, *Visits to the Blessed Sacrament* (*Les Visites au Saint Sacrement*, Éd. Saint Paul)

AL   Compendium, *Alphonse de Liguori, pasteur et Docteur*, Beauchesne

HSE   Théodule Rey-Mermet, CSsR, *Un homme pour les sans-espoir*, Nouvelle Cité

LM   Théodule Rey-Mermet, CSsR, *Moral Choices: The Moral Theology of Saint Alphonsus Liguori*, Liguori Publications, Liguori, MO, 1998 (*La Morale selon Saint Alphonse de Liguori*, Cerf)

SSL   Théodule Rey-Mermet, CSsR, *Saint Alphonsus Liguori: Tireless Worker for the Most Abandoned*, New City Press, 1989 (*Le Saint des Siècle des Lumières*, Nouvelle Cité)

DAY ONE

Go Make a Closed Retreat

FOCUS POINT

We are given the opportunity to spend these fifteen days of retreat with Saint Alphonsus as our spiritual guide. God reaches out to us with his grace, calling us to him; we have the choice—answer him or ignore this call. Let us seek solitude, walk in the presence of God, welcome him, listen to him, and follow him. Let God's grace rain upon us!

Those who have read Saint Francis de Sales' *Introduction to the Devout Life* have met Glycera, the flowerseller. She "knows just how to diversify the arrangement and mixture of flowers so much that, with the same flowers, she was able to make a great variety of bouquets" (chapter one of the first part). From this point of view, many of the saints are remarkable "flower merchants": with the same flowers that bloom by the breath of the Holy Spirit, they realize unique and ravishing bouquets. It is enough just to glance at their lives in order to breathe in the per-

fume of the Gospel there. That is what we are going to do with
Saint Alphonsus Liguori, "the Francis de Sales of Italy," all
throughout these fifteen days of prayer. And first, let us open
with a letter he wrote at the end of his life, a letter in which he
evokes the importance of spiritual retreats to Christians:

> My young friend, you asked me how to chose a profes-
> sion. Go make a closed retreat. Don't expect an angel to
> come to you to show you what career you must choose to
> correspond with what God wants for you. The Spiritual
> Exercises have first been instituted to clarify career choices,
> for each person's salvation is dependent upon this
> choice…. I will confide something to you: I am very at-
> tached to closed retreats, for I owe my conversion and
> the resolution I took to devote myself to God to them.

Alphonsus had the experience of going on retreats: they left their
mark on his life, especially when he was young. We know that his
mother was a pious woman; she gave him the taste for prayer.
His father was a convinced Christian: he took Alphonsus with
him at the age of eighteen to make his first closed retreat with the
Jesuit fathers. That was in 1714. He gave himself to God. Thor-
oughly. Then, year after year, he regularly made a retreat, either
with the Jesuits or with the Lazarists, most often during Holy
Week. But, with time, his fervor cooled—at least, that is his opinion: the opinion of a saint involved in a professional, social, and
political life. During the course of an eight-day retreat in Holy
Week, 1722, with the Lazarists, he took himself in hand. Father
Tannoia, the author of his memoirs, noted then that: "Grace pursued him and refused to let go of him—and didn't stop knocking
at the door of his heart. Grace made him see how much he had
forfeited his first love; and that the world didn't even grasp a tiny
acorn (bit) of the parables; that God was put on the back burner
of his feelings; and that he could only sit at the Holy Table as a
guest, satisfied by something else and without desires. That was
the evening rain on soil that was dried out, but not completely

burned. And here was how to recapture the vigor of the seeds of piety that the thorns of passions had begun to choke out. On the spot, the light of God filled Alphonsus completely; he cried over his straying and, resolved, he promised the Lord to leave the path where he had so inconsiderately wandered" (SSL, p. 113).

"Right up until his death, Alphonsus claimed that these Holy Exercises of 1722 had been God's greatest mercy in his life" (SSL, p. 114). The following year, during his Holy Week retreat, he definitively renounced marriage for himself and also his primogeniture. "The young rich man" from Naples, then, had chosen to give away all of his goods...to leave everything behind in order to follow Jesus. Later, when he wrote his *Hymns and Verses*, he remembered:

> O world, offer me everything, your offer will be in vain; /
> Go, throw the object of their desires to the senseless, /
> Foolish drunkenness of the century, guilty pleasures, / You
> will not have my heart; another Good enchains it...
> (SSL, p. 113–4).

Alphonsus led others on this path of the Gospel. Thus, after the 1723 retreat, a handful of friends decided, along with him, to together make a "monastic" retreat of three or four days every month, away from Naples. Later, having become the founder of a religious missionary institute, he wanted each of his houses to become a retreat house. And quite often, in poor communities, the young religious of his congregation would put their own personal rooms at the disposal of those who came to follow the Spiritual Exercises and make a retreat, whether they were laypersons or religious. His conviction about the importance of retreats was strong. He wrote the following:

> After the grace of baptism and that of a happy death, there is none greater than that of a good retreat.

Saint Alphonsus insisted upon the following conditions for a true retreat: solitude, leaving everything behind for God, walk in his presence, plunge into the desert with the Lord. "The desert is beautiful...what embellishes it is that it hides an oasis here and there," said the Little Prince of Saint Exupéry (1890–1944). This oasis, where Alphonsus found the living water during a retreat, was the Word of God, the Word made flesh, the Son of Mary. He welcomed him, listened to him, and started to follow him.

AND US, TODAY?

Obviously, Alphonsus had been very conscious of the importance of times filled with strong personal evangelization that constitute retreats. Today, he calls upon us to give time to God. Not only each day, but equally, each year, for a few days...as Jesus did when he dedicated entire days and nights to God in the desert before committing himself to the apostolic life...then, a night of prayer before choosing the Twelve...and long hours in the garden of Gethsemane, after the Last Supper, before entering into the mystery of the paschal time of his death and resurrection.

However, Alphonsus does not propose a rigorous and precise program in the style of Saint Ignatius of Loyola's Exercises; he leaves the retreat participant very free, on the condition that he makes a true retreat. Saint Alphonsus's spirituality, in effect, is a *spirituality of truth and simplicity*, or moral honesty (whatever is worth doing is worth doing well) and of a search for what is essential (he had an extreme dislike for the style of the "savants," long and complicated sentences that confused the little people). If retreats affected his life so much, it was because he had made true retreats. Today, he invites us to do our fifteen days of prayer with him like a mini-retreat at home. What type of retreat? Certainly not a retreat where we only think of ourselves. Certainly not a retreat of wasted time where we set ourselves up comfortably in silence like millionaires on vacation: we read spiritual books; we entertain nice thoughts, but don't aim for any objective for the retreat. We pretend: we devote ourselves to our work with all of our spirit instead of letting the Holy Spirit work within us. It is a temptation: that of the hypocritical Pharisee.

Perhaps a good retreat for a year? That is the traditional rhythm. A good retreat...for a year, a little like we do when we make a snack to hold us until the next meal. But what we must do is allow ourselves to be fed and transformed by the Lord in order to better be able, as a result, to work with him to change the world. That is what a good retreat is: we don't make a retreat for ourselves, we make a retreat to become a better worker in the world, in service to others.

And why not a retreat for life? Isn't that an exceptional retreat—one which changes one's personality. From time to time, in fact, the Lord offers this grace. Such retreats are rare. Many retreat participants, however, have had some radiant experiences; for example, the prophet Elijah in the desert, Saint Alphonsus in Naples (in 1722), and so many others, before and after them. Why not you? Why not today?

"I start today...." Alphonsus liked this formula. Without a doubt, he inherited it from Saint Philip Neri and he repeated it often. It can help us to put ourselves on the path at the threshold of these fifteen days of prayer, fifteen days for God, fifteen days with Alphonsus, fifteen days with Jesus and Mary, fifteen days to discover with what love we have been loved, fifteen days of a mini-retreat at home in order to better respond to this love by striving more to "continue Jesus' mission," there where we live. Humbly, joyously.

My Jesus, with the Samaritan woman, I say to you:
"Give me some of that water."
Give me the water of your love so that I forget the
earth and live for you alone, a loving Infinity!
My soul is dry soil that only produces the brambles
and thorns of sin: deem to water it with the waters of
your grace so that it will bring you some fruit,
fulfill some glorious works for you before death
removes me from this world.

O Source of living water, O my Sovereign Good,
how many times I have left you for the muddy waters
that have deprived me of your love! Ah!
May I be dead rather than offend you! In the future,
I want to seek only you, O my God!
Lend me your help and make me faithful to you.
O Mary, my Hope, always keep me under the cloak
of your protection. Amen (VS, pp. 308–9).

REFLECTION QUESTIONS

What emotions am I feeling as I begin this spiritual retreat with Saint Alphonsus as my guide? Fear? Excitement? Anticipation? Am I open to allowing the Holy Spirit to work within me during these fifteen days? Dear God, allow me to abandon my regrets and anger toward the past; ease my anxieties toward the future; be with me here and now, that I may love you in the present moment.

DAY TWO

I Was a Lawyer

FOCUS POINT

Alphonsus was a lay apostle before he sought the religious life. In his house, in his city, Alphonsus lived the Gospel as a lawyer, applying the Gospel to his profession in a practical manner, and affecting those around him with his deep spirituality and love for God. As a lawyer, Alphonsus served God by serving his fellow man, especially the poor, the sick, and the imprisoned. For Alphonsus, holiness was available to everyone.

In 1779, Saint Alphonsus reminded one of his subjects, someone who was more ambitious than competent, of the following: "I was a lawyer..." (*Lettere* II, p. 495). This little phrase reminds us of his old profession and first apostolate. Alphonsus had been a lawyer at the same time as he was a lay apostle. He had, at that time, even wanted to make himself totally available to this apostolate. There is no other explanation, it seems, for his commitment to "celibacy for the Kingdom" from 1722 onwards.

At that time, he was not thinking of becoming a priest; the city of Naples had thousands of priests. What good could yet another priest do? But a Christian layperson, engaged in such an apostolate, could make a difference, in all areas.

Alphonsus, the lawyer, was *an apostle in his own house*. At the process for his canonization, Father Tannoia pointed out how the young Alphonsus had converted his Muslim slave. However, he converted him without proselytism, without asking anything of him, simply by "what he was," by the way he lived. His slave, Abdhalla, gave no other explanation for his conversion than this simple confidence: "I want to be Christian because of my master: this is surely a true religion that makes him live with such virtue, piety, and goodness for me" (SSL, p. 110).

Alphonsus, the lawyer, was *an apostle in his own milieu*, in his relationships. He had friends. They were very important to him. They were faithful friends, companions in prayer whom he often found, in the evenings, at the hour for adoration, before the Blessed Sacrament and, each month, for a short retreat: they took the time there to reflect, pray, share, and sing together. Later, some of them would become his mission companions.

Alphonsus was *an apostle in the city*. Certainly he loved life, he liked to play cards, go to the theater, and, above all, he loved music. But he didn't only think of himself. He was committed in service to others as shown by his presence in numerous Christian associations which came to be called "confraternities." In September 1705, he joined the Confraternity of Young Noblemen. In August 1715, after having finished his "articling" as a lawyer, he joined the Doctors of the Visitation, whose apostolic duties included visiting and caring for three hundred sick patients from the Naples Hospital for the Incurable. Father Berruti wrote: "He went there several times a week and, when there, he made beds, changed clothes, prepared medications, bandaged sores, and gave all the services he was able to the patients without allowing himself to get disgusted because of the foul smell, nausea, or rebuffs by the patients themselves. And he performed these services with such a spiritual joy and respect that, visibly, it was Jesus Christ

whom he served and honored in the person of these sad people"
(SSL, p. 107).

Another confraternity, that of Holy Mary of Mercy, took him
to care for prisoners: he visited and accompanied those who were
condemned to death. He took collections in the streets of Naples
for their families, he welcomed the pilgrim or visiting priests to
the confraternity's inn, and, in a small hospital, he cared for the
indigent priests. This isn't counting the visits he made to those in
prison, often accompanied by the offer of a good meal.

As well as his humanitarian and charitable works, he was
also involved in political and social activities in service to the city.
From the age of fourteen, Alphonsus took charge of his seat in
the Portanova district council which the Liguori family held by
social (since they were of the nobility) right. From 1710 to 1723,
his name can be seen in the meeting minutes. During these meetings, with his colleagues, he participated in the management of
municipal problems: property registration, taxes, welfare, price
controls, purchases and sales, communal rights, ecclesiastical benefits, and so on.

But Alphonsus was first and foremost a lay missionary, in
service to the Gospel at the heart of his profession. The care he
brought to exercise his profession was irreproachable. To this end,
he wrote twelve "commandments" for a lawyer, put them on a
card, and often meditated on them:

1. One must never accept unjust cases because they are bad for
   one's conscience and one's reputation.
2. One must never defend a case with illicit and unjust means.
3. One must not load one's client with unnecessary expenses. A
   lawyer has the obligation to issue a refund if this has been the
   case.
4. One must deal with a client's case with the same care with
   which one deals with one's own.
5. One must study the files in order to draw valid arguments for
   the defense of the case.
6. The delays and carelessness of lawyers can be damaging to

their clients, and the latter must be compensated lest justice is sinned against.

7. A lawyer must implore God for help in his defense, because God is the first protector of justice.

8. A lawyer who accepts many cases which are beyond his ability, his strength, and his time (which will often be lacking for the preparation of the defense) is not to be praised.

9. Justice and honesty are the inseparable companions of Catholic lawyers; in fact they must always be treasured like the apple of their eye.

10. A lawyer who loses a case through negligence must take upon himself the compensation of his client for damages.

11. In defending a case one must be truthful, sincere, respectful, and rational.

12. Finally, the requisites for a lawyer are knowledge, diligence, truth, faithfulness, and justice (SSL, pp. 95–6).

In short, at the age of twenty-three, in the midst of complete professional success, Alphonsus's attitude was one of a layperson committed to serve man: his clients and fellow citizens, but especially the poor people (the sick, prisoners, those who were condemned to death and their families). To be a good Christian, for him, was not to be a monk, priest or bishop, have apparitions or make miracles; it was to follow Jesus on the paths of the Gospel, to continue his work of salvation in the midst of the world. He already felt it: holiness is available to everyone, it is proposed for all. And he already had realized this portrait of a Christian that Saint John Chrysostom had outlined: "Let us imitate the apostles' virtues…it was not their miracles that made them apostles, it was the holiness of their lives. In fact, when the Lord wanted to outline the portrait of his disciples, he said: 'This is what people will recognize in you to see that you are my disciples….' Will it only be in the prodigies that these traits will operate? In the dead that arise? Not at all! But to what then? 'People will know that you are my disciples through the love you have for each other.' Yet love is not a matter for miracles, but simply one of virtue. Why look any further? The Lord himself depicted the disciples as having only one characteristic, that of love."

AND US, TODAY?

In his family, his relationships, and in his city, Alphonsus, a young layperson, was committed in service to his brothers and sisters in a battle without limits for justice and love, particularly within the exercise of his profession, but also in the entirety of his life, even in his leisure activities. Is this not the same call that Vatican Council II makes to us?

> Secular duties and activities belong properly although not exclusively to laymen. Therefore acting as citizens in the world, whether individually or socially, they will keep the laws proper to each discipline, and labor to equip themselves with a genuine expertise in their various fields. They will gladly work with men seeking the same goals.... Laymen should also know that it is generally the function of their well-formed Christian conscience to see that the divine law is inscribed in the life of the earthly city... (*Gaudium et Spes*, no. 43).

Are we aware that, with Jesus and through him, we are "the people who belong to God," this "priestly people" whose vocation it is to offer themselves with Christ, to proclaim the marvels of his message and passage amongst us? Do we show solidarity with those who have been baptized, those "who are royal, priestly, and holy people" and who need, in service to him, following the apostles, not only bishops and religious, but also lay people committed to their professions?

In the same way as the Gospel, and later Vatican Council II, reminds us, Saint Alphonsus invites us to a missionary spirituality, a spirituality of Nazareth, with respect to our professional activities.

Following this call, what is our place in the ever-present fight for justice, peace, and love? Do we want to serve mankind through our profession, visit the sick, be a servant of peace, take up our part of the responsibility in social and political activities in the area where we live...?

> O Word Incarnate, you made yourself become man
> to kindle divine love in our hearts:
> and how could you have met with such
> ingratitude in our hearts?
> You have spared nothing to make yourself loved;
> you have even gone so far as to sacrifice
> your blood and your life for us:
> and how, then, can people still remain so ungrateful?
> Perhaps they don't know it? Yes, they know it,
> and they believe that, for them,
> you have come down from heaven to take on human
> flesh and load yourself with their miseries;
> they know that, for their love, you have led a life of
> continual pain and embraced an ignominious death;
> and how, then, can they explain that they live in
> complete oblivion of your extreme goodness?
> They love their relatives, friends,
> they even love their animals; if they receive any sign of
> love from their animals, they quickly reward it;
> yet towards you alone,
> they are so loveless and ungrateful.
> But alas, what can I say?
> By accusing them, I am my own accuser,
> I have treated you even worse than anyone.
> But your goodness encourages me;
> I know that it has supported me for a long time in
> order to pardon me and inflame me with your love,
> provided that I will repent and love you.
> Yes, my God, I do wish to repent; and I grieve with
> my whole soul for having offended you;
> I want to love you with my whole heart.

*I am well aware, my Redeemer, that my heart is no
longer worthy to welcome you
since it has forsaken you to love creatures; but,
at the same time, I see, in spite of my treason,
that you are willing to have it again, and with all of the
strength of my will, I dedicate it and present it to you.
Inflame it, then, completely with your divine love;
and, from this day onward,
grant that it may love nothing other than you,
O Infinite Goodness, worthy of an infinite love.
I love you, my Jesus; I love you, O Sovereign Good!
I love you, only love of my soul!
O Mary, my Mother,
you are the mother of fair love...
obtain for me the grace to love my God;
my hope is in you. Amen (N, pp. 139–40).*

REFLECTION QUESTIONS

Do I allow the Gospel message to penetrate every part of my life
(work, leisure, "down time") like Saint Alphonsus did? In what
ways do I affect those around me with the way I live and speak
the Gospel message? How can I improve upon this? What areas
of my life do I tend to keep separate from the sacred for one
reason or another? Might I invite God into these "darker" areas
of my life?

DAY THREE

Farewell to the Courts!

FOCUS POINT

We cannot fully put our faith and hope in the law of man. Like Alphonsus discovered as a lawyer, this justice is corruptible and easily swayed. We must entrust ourselves to the mercy and love of our heavenly Father. His love, his justice, his mercy, his law cannot be tainted. He is the greatest good; there is nothing greater to which we can give ourselves. If we trust in something less than God, we must remove ourselves from its false promises immediately and, like Saint Alphonsus, embrace the unwavering love of God.

Anyone who travels to Naples can visit the courthouse where Saint Alphonsus successfully pled his legal cases. They can go and pray in the chapel where he prayed, and could also stop and read the commemorative plaque in honor of "Saint Alphonsus Liguori, Doctor of the Church, former lawyer of this Naples Court." Naples remembers him. Yet we understand nothing of the story and spirituality of Saint Alphonsus if we do not remember his extraordinary professional competence and universal knowledge. Alphonsus Liguori, the noble knight, received such brilliant and solid training since it was the Century of Enlightenment. An accomplished scholar, he knew Greek, Latin, Spanish, and French as well as his maternal tongue. Open to the fine arts, he excelled in music and painting. Not just an amateur, but a professional who studied with the masters. At the age of sixteen, he received his Doctorate in both Civil and Ecclesiastical Law. At the age of eighteen, he became a lawyer. He pursued it for a period of eight years; he lost none of his cases, except the last in which he was undeniably the victim of a grave injustice.

In just a few lines, his best hagiographer, Father Théodule Rey-Mermet, summed up this very complex story:

> It concerned an international case in which Emperor Charles VI himself was involved and in which 600,000 ducats were at stake. It pitted the Neapolitan Duke Philippe Orsini di Gravine (the nephew of Pope Benedict XIII) against the Grand Duke of Tuscany, Cosmo III di Medici. Orsini has entrusted his case to the one who, in spite of his youth, was already considered to be one of the best lawyers in the kingdom—Don Alphonsus Liguori. In spite of opposing evidence, obviously dishonest, Alphonsus pled against the document and for equity. But influence from high political concerns had spoken before him; the judges in which he had confidence, starting with Caravita, allowed themselves to be bought off. When the trial came to its end, probably at the end of July 1723, the die had been cast; the eloquence of the lawyer and the evidence weighed less than a feather (counted very little). Hopping mad, disgusted with the judges whom he believed to have integrity, ashamed of the robe he had worn for the past ten years or so, Alphonsus tore it from his shoulders and left the courthouse forever, never to return, while repeating to himself: "World, I know you…farewell to the courts!" (HSE, pp. 35–6).

Returning to his room, he locked himself in, refusing all food. He was a broken man, blinded. He was blind also about his future. He finally came out to quell his mother's tears. But we would never see him again at the courthouse. In the meantime, he prayed: "Lord, what do you want me to do?"

The answer was not long in coming. A few days later, August 29, Naples was celebrating a joyous occasion, the thirty-second birthday of the Empress Isabelle, the wife of Charles VI. The young Alphonsus Liguori was invited to the king's court. He refused to go. Just the day before, he had discharged his clients. That day, instead of going to the king's court, he went to the Hospital for Incurable Patients where his devotion was usually practiced. It was there that the Lord awaited him. As soon as he arrived, he sensed an urgent call: "Leave the world! Give everything to me!" He continued caring for the sick, but the call was insistent. Then Alphonsus responded: "Here I am, Lord! I have resisted your grace for too long. Do with me what you will!" From there, he went to pray in the Church of the Redemption of the Captives, dedicated to Our Lady of Mercy. After having prayed to the Madonna, the young Alphonsus gave himself totally to the Lord, in an irrevocable manner. In order to underline his commitment, he stood up, removed the sword that signified him as a nobleman and placed it on the Altar of the Blessed Virgin. The date was August 29, 1723. Throughout his entire life, he remembered this day which he called "the day of his conversion." Never did he return to Naples without making a visit in thanksgiving to his benefactress. One day, when he was showing an image of Our Lady of Mercy, he said, "It was she who delivered me from the world and made me enter into the ecclesiastical profession."

AND US, TODAY?

Alphonsus's attitude was like that of Abraham: his spirituality was a spirituality of exodus. He left his own land for a land that God showed him. The noble knight of yesteryear, revolted by injustice, swung into another world, the world of the poor: he would be a priest, Jesus' priest, a lawyer for the Lord's mercy and servant of God's forgiveness for sinners.

And us? Where are we with respect to this love that gives priority to the poor, reminding us of Saint Alphonsus, who was in perfect agreement with the Gospel? It is a call that Vatican Council II brings up again:

> The joys and the hopes, the griefs and the anxieties of the men of this age, especially those who are poor or in any way afflicted, these are the joys and hopes, the griefs and anxieties of the followers of Christ. Indeed, nothing genuinely human fails to raise an echo in their hearts... (*Gaudium et Spes*, no. 1).

Even if we haven't experienced the same problems as Saint Alphonsus, it is no less true that the Gospel, today, invites us to swing away from the world of riches into which we have been born and enter into the world of the poor where the Lord awaits the young rich people we are: "...There is still one thing lacking. Sell all that you own and distribute the money to the poor...then come, follow me" (Lk 18:22).

May our prayer unite with that of Saint Alphonsus and commit us, following his example, to the road of exodus. The call, "come, follow me," is always a call to choose the world of the poor, and to get onto the road for a long journey...towards the land that the Lord will show us, day after day.

O Eternal Word!
You spent thirty-three years in sweat and suffering,
you gave your blood and your life for our salvation:
in short, you spared nothing to make us love you.
Then how can there be people who know this
and yet do not love you?
O God, I am one of these ingrates.
I see the wrong I have done:
O my Jesus, have pity on me.

I offer you this ungrateful heart of mine—
ungrateful but repentant.
Yes, above every other evil, my dear Redeemer,
I repent for having scorned you.
I repent, and I am sorry with all of my heart.
My soul, you love a God who is bound
like a criminal for you,
a God scourged like a slave for you,
a God who made himself a king of scorn for you,
in short, one who was executed as if he were a villain.
Yes, my Savior, my God, I do love you.
Always remind me of everything that you suffered for me,
so that I may never again forget to love you.
Ropes that bound Jesus, bind me to Jesus;
thorns that crowned Jesus,
wound me with love for Jesus; nails that pierced Jesus,
nail me to the cross of Jesus,
so that I may live and die united to Jesus. Amen
(AA, p. 11–12).

REFLECTION QUESTIONS

To what things less than God do I sometimes give myself over? What empty promises of fulfillment, what anxieties, what obstacles distract me from following God at all times? Do financial concerns, fighting within the family, or anxiety over what tomorrow might bring wrestle away from me the attention, trust, and energy I owe to my Creator? What types of prayer might I employ to maintain my focus on the center of my life, my God and Father?

DAY FOUR

I Am a Priest

FOCUS POINT

God calls each one of us to a specific vocation; that is, we are called to live his Word and preach that Word in a way specific to who we are as individuals. Some, like Alphonsus, are called to the religious life, some to the business world, others to family life, and so on. Each vocation has its own obstacles, opportunities, challenges, and particular joys. In each of these vocations to which we are called, God wants us to be happy, at peace with who we are, as we express our great love for him in our unique service.

It is clear that our eternal salvation depends mainly on the choice of a profession. Father Louis de Grenade called this choice the "mainspring of life"; in a clock, if the mainspring is faulty, the entire clock is out of order; in the same way, with respect to our salvation, if we miss our vocation, our entire life is ruined. If we want to assure our salvation, then we must embrace the profession to which God calls us, for only there has he prepared the effective help that is needed for our salvation. Saint Paul tells us that: "Each of us receives a particular gift from God...." Thus, when the Lord calls someone, he must obey, and obey without delay (HSE, p. 39).

T his appeared in Saint Alphonsus's *Consideration on a Religious Vocation*, a book that he published in 1750. In 1723, he was already putting it into practice. In the same way, before writing his book, *Prayer to Know His Vocation*, he made his own prayer:

> *My God, I am this poor sinner who,*
> *in the past, had so much scorn for you.*
> *But, at this moment,*
> *I love you and cherish you more than ever.*
> *I want to love only you.*
> *You want me completely for yourself and*
> *I want to be totally yours.*
> *"Speak, Lord, your servant is listening...."*
> *Make me aware of what you expect of me.*

And, in 1723, he registered at the high seminary in Naples, as a day student. There, he studied theology under the direction of a great master, Don G. Torni. There, he also met two spiritual authors, Saint Teresa of Ávila and Saint Francis de Sales, who would affect his life and whom he would cite abundantly in his own writings. For three years he pursued his commitments to the sick, continuing to visit and care for them regularly. Among the practicing pastoral work teams proposed by the seminary, he decided to join the Association for Propaganda, currently called the Apostolic Missions, run by a group of diocesan priests. Thus, beginning in November 1724, as a simple cleric, he took part in his first mission, in Santo Eligio, in the poorer neighborhoods of Naples: "A special date for him, for the Redemptorists, for the

Church...and already a sign from God: he had first been sent to the poorest, to the most abandoned people" (HSE, p. 44).

On Saturday, April 6, 1726, Alphonsus took a new step towards the priesthood: he was ordained a deacon. From that time on, he could serve at the two tables: the table of the Eucharist and the table of the Word. In his first sermon, the former lawyer, invited to preach the adoration of the forty hours, commented on a text from the Book of Isaiah (64) which we find echoed in his *Novena for Christmas*, which he published in 1758:

> The prophet wrote, before the divine Word had even come to earth: "Oh, that you would tear open the heavens and come down so that the mountains would quake at your presence...and the fire causes the water to boil..." (Isa 64:1, 2), that is, you would deem to leave the heavens and descend here to become man amongst us! Men would surmount all obstacles, all difficulties, in observing your laws and councils; ...even the most frozen souls would be transformed by your blessed love! In fact, after the Incarnation of the Word, how brilliantly has the fire of divine love shone to many loving souls! And it may indeed be asserted, without fear of contradiction, that God was more beloved in one century after the coming of Jesus Christ than in the entire forty preceding centuries. How many youths, nobles, even how many monarchs, have left wealth, honors, and even their kingdoms to seek the retreat of the desert or the cloister, so that there, in poverty and obscure seclusion, they might the more unreservedly give themselves up to the love of their Savior! How many martyrs have faced torment and death with joy, smiles on their lips! How many young virgins have refused the proffered hands of the great ones of this world in order to go and die for Jesus Christ, and to repay the affection to God who became man in his plan to die for their salvation! (N, p. 136).

Alphonsus Liguori was ordained a priest on December 21, 1726. He was thirty years old. He had chosen the world of the little ones, the poor, the sick, people of all kinds who were excluded: this world that he only intermittently approached in the past to make a few gestures of charity, sincere, but isolated, had definitely become his own. This commitment was one of love. Furthermore, love would be the preferred theme of his writings. The following text, published in Naples in 1766, in his book, *The Way of Salvation*, is proof of this:

> The Apostle said: "The love of Christ urges us on" (2 Cor 5:14). Oh my Redeemer, you have died for the love of men, but why do men not love you back? Because they live their lives without thinking of the death you have endured in order to save them. If they thought about it, how could they live without loving you? Saint Francis de Sales said: "Knowing that Jesus Christ, the true God, loved us so much, to the point of suffering death on the cross for us, do we not, as a result, feel our hearts in a vice, held forcibly, love squeezed from them by a kind of constraint that is as powerful as it is loving?" And it is precisely this gentle pressure exerted on our hearts that Saint Paul speaks about when he says: "The love that Jesus Christ has shown us, urges us on, forces us to love him."
>
> My beloved Lord, in the past, I have scorned you, but now I hold you in esteem and love you more than my own life. My most vivid pain is the one I feel when I remember the many offenses I have committed against you, O my love! Pardon me, O Jesus; draw my whole heart to you, so that, from now on, I will want only you, seek only you, sigh after no other but you (VS, pp. 64–5).

Alphonsus loved Christ, he loved the world of mankind, above all, the poorest people: he gave himself to Christ, he gave himself to his new mission. Fully! He chose to be a priest of salvation in order to continue the salvific work of Christ. But at what price?

That of quality. Before, when he was a lawyer, Alphonsus had made himself a life plan (see Day Two). Today, having become a priest, he has made himself a new plan—one that gives rules for his priestly conduct:

1. As a priest, my dignity is greater than that of the angels; I must therefore be entirely pure and, as far as possible, an angelic man.
2. At Mass, God obeys my voice, and I must obey his, the inspirations he sends, and also the voice of my superiors.
3. The holy Church honors me, and I must honor the Church with the holiness of my life, my zeal, my hard work, and dignified behavior.
4. I offer Jesus Christ to the Eternal Father, and I must clothe myself with the virtues of Jesus Christ and must never neglect to prepare myself to meet the Holy of Holies.
5. The Christian people look on me as a minister of reconciliation with God; therefore I must be always close to God's heart and never lose his friendship.
6. Virtuous people rely on my example to help them become holy; therefore I must always give them a good example.
7. Poor sinners are waiting for me to free them from the death of sin; I must do this through prayer, through example, through word and work.
8. I need fortitude and courage to overcome the world, the flesh, and the devil, and with the help of God's grace, I will prevail.
9. I must master the wisdom to defend our holy faith, combat errors, and banish ungodliness.
10. I must never act out of human weakness and I must learn to shun worldly friendships as I would the devil; since such behavior dishonors the priesthood.
11. I must loathe ambition and self-interest as plagues on the priestly life: many priests have endangered the faith through ambition.
12. I must be charitable and never thoughtless; I must be prudent and reserved, especially with women—but not proud, harsh, or scornful.

13. If I wish to please God, recollection, intense desire, solid virtue, and the practice of prayer must occupy my time constantly.
14. I must seek only the glory of God, the sanctification of my soul,
and the salvation of my neighbor, even at the cost of my life.
15. As a priest, I must inspire virtue and glorify the supreme and
eternal priest, Jesus Christ (SSL, pp. 164–5).

Alphonsus was a very competent and well-read priest. He had
benefited from the best human training available in his era with
the best tutors. In the past, he had worked to become a law professional and an orator who served justice. Now, he worked to
become a lawyer for God and sinners, an orator of the Word of
God: his talents, and they were immense, were put into service
for the Gospel. First, he used his talent as a preacher. He liked to
say: "It is by preaching, and that alone, that Jesus Christ undertook the conversion of mankind; it is then through preaching that
it must be pursued. What is important is that we preach about
the crucified Christ" (SSL, p. 585).

Alphonsus was a zealous priest. He evangelized with enthusiasm, happy to collaborate with the Lord for the salvation of the
world. He demanded this zeal and enthusiasm from all of the
priests he encountered throughout his life. After having taken
special care with the spiritual training of the priests in his own
diocese and in the missionary institute he had founded, did he not
address them severely in his book, *The Selva (Dignity and Duties
of the Priest With Two Rules of Life for Secular Priests)*?

In the world there are, at the same time, both many and
few priests; there are many in name, but few in reality.
The world is filled with priests, but there are few who
seek to truly be such through their work, that is, who
fulfill the duties and obligations of a priest for the salvation of souls.

The dignity of a priest is great…. Is there any greater
dignity than working with God to save the souls he has

redeemed? The Lord wanted the priests to be the saviors of the world.... In his work of creation, God had no one to help him; but in the mystery of the Redemption of the world, he would like to rely upon his collaborators.

Alphonsus was a happy priest. "*Allegramente!* With joy! With gladness!" Often, he would repeat these words of Saint Philip Neri. He was truly happy to be a priest. He was happy to evangelize, happy to preach. Tannoia stated: "To be invited to preach was the same as being invited to a celebration: he joyously accepted with a joyful willingness." And everyone called upon him: "As a priest, he saw himself soon overrun with so much work that he didn't have time to catch his breath. One ministry wasn't yet finished and he undertook another. The rectors of the churches argued over who would be the first to have his faithful parishioners benefit from Alphonsus's preaching skills" (HSE, p. 54). He accepted with a good heart, convinced, as he would later write, that "if a sinner incurred damnation because he had no one to preach the Word of God to him, the Lord will make the priests who could have done it, but didn't, accountable for it."

AND US, TODAY?

Devotion to Saint Alphonsus doesn't come to us as a hazy and sentimental mysticism; it is of an adult, a free man, who loved, gave everything, who gave of himself. One characteristic of his spirituality was his love for a job well done.

As a priest, his spiritual model was that of the Good Shepherd who sets out in search for his lost sheep, who gives his life so that they would have life in abundance. As an ordained priest, he strived to completely fulfill his mission: he must first lead his "Lord's sheep," the people of whom he had the charge, towards "the green pastures" of the Word of God. For that, he considered it very important to develop the talents he had received, and to reach a certain high level of competence through hard work in all of the areas of his apostolic activities.

And us, are we sufficiently conscious of the talents that we have received? Do we see to it that we develop them to put them into service for the Gospel?

Are we zealous servants, enthusiastic baptized believers of the Gospel? Are we people who show the joy of the resurrection on our faces? Too often, are we not sad and mute witnesses?

Let us pray for the priests to fulfill their mission and for the Church for priestly vocations, which are so very badly needed.

Lord Jesus, you, who, in order to save souls,
had given your life, give enlightenment and your love
to as many priests who could convert the multitudes of
sinners and sanctify the world if only they preach your
word without vanity and with simplicity,
just like you and your disciples had preached.
But, instead of preaching about you,
they preach about themselves.
Thus, the world is filled with preachers
but the souls are still going to hell.
Lord, heal this immense scourge which,
because of the preachers, weighs on your Church.
Amen (SSL, pp. 467–8).

REFLECTION QUESTIONS

How do I view my working life? Do I see it as a vocation to which I have been called by God? Do I see the relationship between my working life—and all the small and sometimes tedious tasks that comprise it—and the Gospel proclaimed by Jesus Christ? Might I pray that God will open my eyes to the myriad moments I often overlook in my working life that are opportunities to show others the great love and mercy God has for his people?

DAY FIVE

Saints Among the Cabbies of Naples!

FOCUS POINT

The ideal spiritual life consists of loving God with our whole heart, and everything else will follow. Holiness is not reserved for those in monasteries or convents. Holiness is available to all of us, each and every one. God gives his grace to all of us, regardless of social standing, vocation, or appearance. Everyone must be made aware of the fact that holiness is theirs if they seek it; no one should feel that they are unworthy of God and his grace.

The sanctity and perfection of a soul consists entirely in loving Jesus Christ, our God, our Sovereign Good, and our Redeemer. Jesus said: "Whoever loves me, shall be loved by my Eternal Father" (see Jn 14:21, 23) for "the Father himself loves you, because you have loved me..." (Jn 16:27).

*Some, says Saint Francis de Sales, argue that perfection con-
sists in an austere life, others in prayer, others in frequenting the
sacraments, others in almsgiving. But they deceive themselves:
perfection consists in loving God with our whole heart.*

*The apostle Paul wrote, "above all, clothe yourselves with
love, which binds everything together in perfect harmony" (Col
3:14). Love unites and preserves all the virtues that make a person perfect. Hence Saint Augustine said: "Love God, and do
whatever you please," because a soul that loves God is taught by
that same love never to do anything to displease God, and to
leave nothing undone that may please him.*

*Doesn't God deserve all our love? He has loved us from all
eternity: "I have loved you with an everlasting love" (Jer 31:3).
Look, says the Lord, I was the first to love you. You were not yet
in the world; the world itself wasn't even there, and I already
loved you. As long as I have been God, I have loved you; as long
as I have loved myself, I have also loved you... (AA, pp. 1–2).*

Right from the first lines of his masterpiece, *The Practice of
the Love of Jesus Christ*, Alphonsus lets us in on the conviction that inhabited him from the first days of his priesthood: holiness is not reserved for the religious or an elite group of virtuous
and cultivated people. No, holiness is offered to everyone, even
the most humble and the poorest. Alphonsus declared it at numerous times, as he did in chapter eight of the same book:

It is a great mistake to say: "God doesn't want everyone to
be a saint." To the contrary, Saint Paul says, "For this is the
will of God, your sanctification…" (1 Thess 4:3). God wants
all of us to be saints, and each one according to his or her
vocation in life: the religious as a religious, lay people as lay
people, the priest as a priest, the married person as married,
the merchant as a merchant, the soldier as a soldier, and so
on, for the other vocations and professions (AA, p. 76).

That is why, as a young priest, Alphonsus left to seek the lost sheep. His friend, Father Tannoia wrote: "Once he was a priest, he spent the majority of his time in the neighborhood where the dregs of the Neapolitan society lived. He was happy to find himself in the midst of the riffraff, those he called the *lazzaroni* (this name makes a reference to the poor Lazarus in one of Jesus' parables) and other little people in varied states of misery and poverty. More than to anyone else, he had given them his heart. And surely, he taught them through his preaching and reconciled them with God through confession. Word traveled across the neighborhood and then all across the city, they came from all around: sinners, scoundrels, that and even more...then they came back. And not only did they stop their sinful ways, they began to pray, contemplate, and soon had no other thought in their heads than loving Jesus Christ" (SSL, pp. 173–4).

Alphonsus welcomed everyone but he went to the people, and the people came to him. Very quickly, he was overwhelmed by the number. Outdoor meetings...it was like the time of the first churches! Here was the program for these meetings, set by Saint Alphonsus, which was so well summed up by his historian: "No vocal prayers, that was an easy method of which he was suspicious—'this people honor me with their lips, but their hearts are far from me' (Mt 15:8). His program included comments upon a maxim from the Gospel, then some instruction on a point of faith; an exhortation for the belief in the holy Sacrament and the Blessed Virgin, and, finally, fifteen minutes of practical meditation on the last days or the Passion of Jesus Christ" (T. Rey-Mermet, "Alphonsus Liguori" in *The History of the Saints and Christian Sainthood*, vol. 9, p. 46, Hachette).

The archbishop of Naples, upon learning of Alphonsus's work among the poor in the roughest sections of town was enthralled and said: "the laity do so much good!" and, for these evenings, put public oratories and chapels at their disposition. That is the origin of the name for these evenings, which were called the Evening Chapels. In fact, each evening, when the workday was over for the men (for the women, their work continued on into the nights…), the *lazzaroni*, masons, barbers, woodworkers, and so on, gathered together in communities of believers. About one hundred people gathered for each Chapel. Alphonsus entrusted the running of these to converted lay people: the priests were only the assistants. There were no forms to fill upon entering in order to be accepted, no dues to pay, no "mandate" received from a priest or a bishop. It was for the lay people who were in charge to invite other lay people in the name of Jesus Christ…encouraged by Alphonsus who had, himself, quite recently been a layperson engaged in the apostolate of his own neighborhood. However, these lay people were not satisfied to just listen to the Gospel and explain it, they put it into practice together: mutual aid and sharing amongst the poor, visits to the sick, a sense of professional conscience restored amongst the thousands of domestics, artisans, laborers, and carpenters. Family money was no longer wasted gambling or drinking. Robbery was replaced by work. Such were the very concrete fruit of these conversions. One of the last causes of Alphonsus's joy, at the end of his life, was to have heard an architect, who was also a friend, say:

> The Evening Chapels? We see that a crowd of people go
> to them and we even have saints amongst the cabbies.
>   Holy cabbies in Naples! Gloria Patri. You have heard
> it correctly, holy cabbies in Naples! (see SSL, p. 625).

In 1798, Tannoia could write that "the Evening Chapels were Alphonsus's (and no one else's) work with his penitents. Today, they number seventy-five, and each recognizes all of the good the little people can draw from them. These people have, as assistants, zealous priests, and their work gives the greatest joy to the archbishops of Naples. To go to these meetings, there is no fee, no officials to meet, nor formalities of any kind. And if someone who attends is a vagrant, lost to crime, that is perfect happiness" (HSE, pp. 71–2).

Two centuries before Pius XI, the Evening Chapels began, under the title "the neighborhood's apostolate for the neighborhood." In the same way, in the middle of the eighteenth century, certain "basic Christian communities" formed, analogous to those which are the hope for the Church in the countries of Africa and Latin America at the present time.

AND US, TODAY?

One characteristic of Saint Alphonsus's spirituality is that it's a "popular spirituality." It addresses itself to everyone across all class or racial boundaries: it is not just reserved for the elite. He never stopped reminding us that everyone could be holy, that is, attain the perfection exacted for us about which Jesus spoke: "Be perfect like your heavenly Father is perfect." This perfection, this "Christification," this edification (don't be afraid of the words) is not only reserved for the privileged few. Furthermore, this holiness that is proposed to everyone is not the fruit of the individual exploits of each person in isolation, but it is the marvelous fruit of the welcome each person gives to the gifts of the Holy Spirit with the help of the community. How does that work? It is interesting to remember the method Saint Alphonsus used for the framework of the Evening Chapels: a priority given to listening to the Word of God, then prayer, and finally, to the devotion to the Eucharist, to the Passion of Jesus and to the Blessed Virgin. Is this method not the one that is still used today?

Furthermore, this method is not "clerical" because Alphonsus entrusted the apostolic responsibilities to lay people.

Where are we with respect to this fraternal trust given to lay people, deacons, priests, and everyone? Where are we with respect to this immense trust in God who wants to save us all, one after another, one for another?

> *O most loving and lovable heart of Jesus,*
> *unhappy is the heart that does not love you!*
> *O God, you died on the cross,*
> *abandoned and wholly bereft,*
> *for the love of your people.*

How, then, can we live so forgetful of your goodness?
O love of God! O human ingratitude!
O you short of memory,
look upon the innocent Lamb of God,
agonizing on the cross and dying for you in order to
satisfy divine justice for your sins,
and so draw you to his love.
Look how, at the same time,
he prays to his heavenly Father to forgive you.
Look at him and love him....May the sorrows of Jesus,
the ignominies of Jesus, the wounds of Jesus,
the death of Jesus, and the love of Jesus
thrust themselves into my heart,
and may their sweet memory remain there forever to
wound me continually and inflame me with love.
I love you, my Jesus, I love you, my Sovereign Good;
I love you, my love, my everything: I love you,
and I want that love for you to last forever.
Never let me leave you or lose you again.
Make me completely yours;
do it through the merits of your death.
In this, I firmly trust.
And I have great confidence, too,
in your intercession, O Mary, my Queen;
make me love Jesus Christ and make me also love you,
my Mother and my Hope! Amen (AA, pp. 68–9).

REFLECTION QUESTIONS

What is my reaction to the "popular spirituality" presented by Saint Alphonsus? Isn't his message exactly the Gospel Jesus Christ lived and preached? God is available to everyone, regardless of class or race, wealth or pedigree. How do I live this "popular spirituality" in my own life? How does this "popular spirituality" preached by Saint Alphonsus affect my own opinions, prejudices, and outlook on the world?

DAY SIX

To Continue the Savior's Mission

FOCUS POINT

The mission of Alphonsus's order was (and is) to bring the Word of God to the poor, "to continue Jesus Christ." No one should feel abandoned by God, or feel separated from the people of God. This is not only the call of the Redemptorists; it is our responsibility—all of us—as servants of God, to reach out to those in need of love and caring, compassion and sharing. As God has loved us, we are called to love others so that they might know his love.

The peasants of Cagliano, a little village in Lucanie (Italy) said: "Christ stopped at Eboli"—they felt so abandoned! Carlo Levi, the author of a book whose title reminds us of this cry of distress, lived there, under house arrest from 1935–6. He heard this cry, he saw this misery. He has told about it. His book, *Christ Stopped at Eboli*, was an event: the film adapted from it was a success. In 1980, the region of Eboli appeared on the news across the globe. Southern Italy had just been ravaged by an earthquake: 100,000 were homeless, thousands were dead! The epicenter had been on the outskirts of Eboli. However, what many people forget is that this same region of Italy, in the eighteenth century, had been the epicenter of a shock wave of another sort: a spiritual one. It shook Alphonsus; it shook the Church. During a mission in this region, Alphonsus uncovered the misery and abandonment of the country people. He was shocked to the bone. For this all happened just a few hours' walk from the capital of the kingdom that was overrun with priests! When Alphonsus returned to Naples, his outlook had changed. God's words incessantly called to him: "…the children beg for food, but no one gives them anything" (Lam 4:4). Who would break the bread of the Word to these "abandoned souls, deprived of spiritual help"? However, it was impossible to think about it for any length of time: the missions went on at an incredible pace in the city and in the kingdom of Naples. Alphonsus gave of himself completely, his health faltered. He fell ill, seriously ill. However, he did recover, but the warning was a serious one and could not be ignored: the doctor prescribed a convalescence in the mountains, immediately!

The summer of 1730 was approaching. His friends invited Alphonsus to rest in the hills that overlooked Scala and Amalfi Bay. With them, he climbed to the top, more than 3,500 feet in altitude. There, one could find the small hermitage of Santa-Maria-dei-Monti (Holy Mary of the Mountains), an ideal site for a convalescence and a splendid panorama. But Alphonsus didn't waste time taking care of himself, nor did he stop to admire the countryside. A crowd of "little people" rushed up towards the chapel. With his companions, he began to catechize peasants and shepherds, preaching to them and hearing their confessions. In short, what Alphonsus had noticed over the period of many years was now evident to him, not only in Eboli, but also "in the vast regions of the kingdom." He wrote about it later in his petition to Benedict XIV in order to obtain approval for his congregation. This situation was not an exception, but the norm for the country people: they were ignored, abandoned by the pastoral works of the time. He who had again recently dreamed of leaving for far-off China, came to discover a China that was closer to home: the Neapolitan countryside! What was his conclusion? Must he not found an institute whose duties would be to respond to this missionary emergency? Alphonsus considered it seriously: he consulted his director and spiritual counselors. Their reply was a formal and unanimous "yes."

In short, on November 2, 1732, Alphonsus, "sure of God's will, spirited himself and gathered his courage. By making a total sacrifice of the city of Naples to Jesus Christ, he offered to live the rest of his days in the pastures and thatched cottages, and to die there, amongst the shepherds and country people." And his historian, Tannoia, solemnly added, a few pages later: "The year 1732 was fixed by God, in advance, for the happy birth of our congregation. Pope Clement XII was in the Vatican and Charles Augustus VI governed the empire and this kingdom of Naples. Alphonsus Liguori, with the blessings of Fathers Fiorillo and Pagano, climbed aboard the peasants' mount; to the insult of his parents and close friends, he left Naples, on the back of a donkey, and took the road to Scala" (SSL, p. 249).

On the back of a donkey! The horse had been the mount of the noblemen. The donkey was the mount of the little people, the mount of the Lord on Palm Sunday. The noble knight no longer existed, Alphonsus made himself poor...just as Jesus did. His project was, as he said numerous times, to "continue Jesus Christ...." It was for that reason that he founded a new institute:

> The aim of this congregation...will be to follow the example of our Savior Jesus Christ in preaching the divine Word to the poor, as he said of himself: "...he has anointed me to bring good news to the poor" (Lk 4:18). This is why the members of the congregation will devote themselves entirely to bringing help to the people scattered over the countryside and the rural hamlets, especially to those most destitute of spiritual assistance...their houses must always be situated outside of the urban areas...in

order to be always ready to move swiftly around the countryside…and to welcome the poor country people… (SSL, p. 376).

"To continue Jesus Christ"—that is Saint Alphonsus's formula. At a time when the spiritualists of his era were content to speak about "imitating Jesus Christ," Saint Alphonsus preferred the expression "to continue Jesus Christ, to continue the mission of Christ the Savior." For him, what was important didn't lie in first seeking his own perfection in a copy of a model; what was important was to attach himself to Christ who, through his death and glorification, continues his mission for the salvation of the world. This implies a choice that took priority: the one to serve the poor, the marginal, the abandoned people. From that, the instructions were clear for his first companions:

If we are presented two missions, one for Naples, and one for the shepherds in the Salerno region, and there are not enough of us to preach both at the same time, it was to the shepherds that we must go first, rescheduling Naples for a later time, for that is the goal of our institute (HSE, p. 154).

Let us notice, however, that the evangelization of the abandoned people, undertaken by Saint Alphonsus and his companions, was not only realized by giving missions to them. Different from the numerous missionaries of the time who, we could say, "passed through like the fog," happy to elicit an emotion with no follow-up or future, Alphonsus insisted upon a calm mission, of a certain duration, careful to bring a catechism to the adults that was within their grasp. Furthermore, Alphonsus asked his companions to set themselves up amidst the poor who they were there to evangelize. Thus, they found themselves in a state of permanent mission to them. That would be the rule adopted by Alphonsus as seen in a text from 1747:

The fundamental purpose of the priests of the Most Holy Redeemer is, in order to continue the example of our common Savior, Jesus Christ, to first employ themselves, through obedience to the bishops, to help those in the countryside who were the most destitute of spiritual assistance...but they would have this absolutely distinctive trait: their houses and churches must always be situated outside of the urban areas and in the center of the dioceses in order to radiate into these regions through their missions and, at the same time, to provide easier access for the poor peasants to the Word of God and the sacraments.

This text reveals an important characteristic of his missionary spirituality: the priority of love for the poor and marginal people. Alphonsus was convinced that he and his companions had been chosen, gathered by Christ to be sent to the poorest and most abandoned people of his flock. But going and giving them missions wasn't enough. In order to "continue" Christ the Savior, it was imperative for the apostle to "set up his tent" amongst them. Alphonsus said it, he wrote it, and he did it. All of his foundations were systematically established among the people in the countryside. In this way, little by little, we become acquainted with what Alphonsus was. He appeared to be:

- *A man of courage*: he was first a priest who was opposed to Jansenism and the rigorousness of his time in the name of the Gospel. Moreover, faced with the spiritual misery of the poor country people, he reacted by mobilizing other priests to go to introduce the Church into their lives, right where they lived.
- *A man of conscience*: certainly, his former profession had given him training in law, as much civil as ecclesiastical, which made him able to analyze the most complex moral cases. But, as a well-read man, he remembered the primacy of conscience when faced with the excess legalism of the moral teachers of his era. Two centuries later, Vatican Council II would bring a

striking confirmation to his ideas: "It is because of his conscience that man perceives and recognizes the injunctions of
the divine law; it is to that which he is held to faithfully follow in all of his activities, in order to reach his goal, which is
God" (*Decree About Religious Freedom*, no. 3).

• *A man of renewal*: Alphonsus was a man for his time, he
discovered the humanism of the Century of Enlightenment,
the importance of art and especially that of music, as well as
technical means of communication: the print shop and his
networks of distribution. He used all of the media of the time:
publishing small pocket books, sketches of holy images, the
composition of spiritual hymns (words and music), reproduc-
tions of his painting of Christ on the cross, and so on. Finally,
Alphonsus, for the Gospel, became the inventor of a new
written language: popular Tuscan. All of this was done so
that the poor could discover the immense love that God has
for mankind, for all mankind.

AND US, TODAY?

Do we have a missionary spirituality like Saint Alphonsus? Have
we made the decision to commune with the will of the love of the
Father, his will for universal salvation? Are we attentive to the
pastoral emergencies?

Have we understood that the formula that Alphonsus and his
companions held so dear, "to continue Jesus Christ," is a formula
of interest to all Christians, for it simplifies and unifies the spiritual life? Alphonsus didn't want a part-time apostolate, but a
full-time one. He didn't want a complicated spirituality, but one
that was simple, unified, in the evangelical style, adapted to the
people.

And us? Are we not too easily satisfied to know a great deal
of things about the Lord rather than do a great deal of things for
him? To know a great deal about the beautiful words to speak to
God rather than speaking to God and commit ourselves in a concrete way to serve him?

Do we care enough to inform our conscience and that of others and respect them?

For us, to continue Jesus Christ and his mission, isn't it a true choice: the one made to be sent to meet the little ones, the sick, and the sinners in order to reveal the love of God to them? Is our missionary spirituality well characterized by the priority of love for the poor, just as Vatican Council II reminded us that the Church should be "the servant of the poor"?

Most lovable heart of my divine Savior,
O heart in love with humankind,
since you love us so tenderly,
O heart worthy of ruling and possessing all our hearts,
how much I want to make everyone understand
the love you feel for them,
and the sweetness you show to those
who love you without reserve!
O Jesus, O my love, here is my will, please accept
this offering and sacrifice that I make to you today.
Let me know what you want from me;
for I wish to do everything with the help of your grace.
Amen (AA, p. 144).

REFLECTION QUESTIONS

How attentive am I to the needs of the poor? Am I drawn to seek them out and serve them? Practically speaking, what volunteer opportunities to work with the poor are available through my church, in my parish, in my city? We are called to be servants of the poor; it is Jesus Christ himself who calls us to serve people in need, and he tells us "do not be afraid" as we seek to do so.

DAY SEVEN

With the Lord, Salvation Is Overflowing

FOCUS POINT

God should inspire love and hope in every one of us; we should not fear and dread God. God's mercy and love are overflowing, and we are all called to drink from the fountain of salvation. Unfortunately, at times, we become so legalistic that religion and its laws become our god, instead of God himself. Jesus freed us from the shackles of legalism; it is up to us to abandon those chains and focus our lives on loving God rather than enslaving our lives to the laws of religion.

Mary was in the habit of praying with the Psalms. In the same way, so did her son, Jesus. Alphonsus did this, as well. In 1774, he published *Explanation of the Psalms and Canticles*, based upon the Italian breviary, to assist priests and monks in their duties to the divine Offices. In 1732, the words from Psalm 130:7,

"For with the Lord…is great power to redeem," fascinated his spirit and heart. We can find them engraved on the first seal of his institute: he designed it himself, around 1747. Such is the motto he chose for his missionaries. Jesus and Mary's initials frame the cross, elevated on three mounds under God's gaze, flanked with the sword and sponge of the Passion, surrounded by an extract from the seventh verse of Psalm 130:

> For with the Lord there is steadfast love,
> and with him is great power to redeem.

To have chosen such a motto in the eighteenth century was to have made a revolutionary choice: so many preachers preached about "the chosen few." This was a motto that declared a war on Jansenism and rigors under all its forms; it believed in abundant redemption, "not only in quantity: many people saved; but in quality: many saints from all areas" (AL, p. 278). We then can understand why Saint Alphonsus wrote his *Moral Theology*: not in any way to split hairs in a few difficult cases, but to help the priests to better fulfill their ministry of reconciliation with their penitents of all ages and from all walks of life:

> This is what the Lord said to the prophet Jeremiah: "See, today I appoint you over nations and over kingdoms, to pluck up and to pull down, to destroy and to overthrow, to build and to plant" (Jer 1:10). He says the same thing to all confessors. They must, in fact, not be satisfied to just remove vices from their penitents, they must also plant virtues in them…. It is very pleasant work for God…to work with these souls who have given themselves completely to him. A perfect soul is worth more in God's eyes that a thousand mediocre ones (AL, p. 276).

This declaration goes along with the evangelical battle that led Alphonsus to save those on the margins of society in his time. He preached love and hope, not a fear of God. He asked that all preachers do the same: "conversions made based on fear don't even last a day. Conversions made based on love last forever."

What we have less proof of concerns those under this same coat of arms who also alluded to extraordinary phenomena that took place on numerous occasions at the monastery in Scala in 1732, during the exposition of the Blessed Sacrament, under the gaze of the religious, and also in the presence of Alphonsus, his companions as well as many bishops and ecclesiastical dignitaries. On this subject, Monsignor Falcoia wrote about what he had seen in the sisters' chapel at Scala, in a letter to Saint Alphonsus on September 11:

> All of the sisters present and their Chaplain (Pietro Romano)...clearly saw, in the holy Eucharist, the holy cross, first black, with, in the middle of it, a resplendent crucified Christ; the cross then became the color of blood; and, finally, white. We observed three rust-colored globes, the instruments of the Passion, some small white clouds and other details. Some of the sisters were overwhelmed; others left the chapel, seized with respect and fear. Finally, all were happy, they had seen authentic confirmation, from God, for the institute and an announcement of the crosses which are never lacking when following Jesus Christ. Nevertheless, for the moment, let us not publicize this; keep it for ourselves—to encourage you in your work and remove all your hesitation (SSL, p. 252).

"Let us not publicize this"—Alphonsus almost never spoke of this. In fact, for a man of his time, in the Century of Enlightenment, he gave a very secondary importance to amazing phenomena: apparitions, visions, and miracles. What interested him was not extraordinary phenomena, but the extraordinary truth of the Word of God, which was full of hope, as expressed in Psalm 130, and the mission he and his companions received to continue the work of the Redeemer by working with spirit and heart with God so that his will of love would triumph:

But our conformity to God's will must be complete, unreserved, and constant; we cannot go back on our word. This is the height of perfection; and this, I repeat, must be the goal of all our works, all our desires, and all our prayers. Some souls given to prayer, upon reading of the ecstasies and raptures of someone like Saint Teresa, Saint Philip Neri, and other saints, dream of reaching this sort of supernatural union. Such longings must be dismissed, because they run counter to humility. If we wish to become saints, we must desire a true union with God, which is to unite our will entirely to his. Saint Teresa writes: "Those who believe that union with God consists in ecstasies, raptures, and enjoyment of him are deceiving themselves. It consists in nothing more or less than subjecting our will to the will of God. This submission is perfect when our will is detached from everything and united only with God's, so that its every movement is what God alone wills" (AA, p. 139).

Alphonsus's spirituality has nothing complex or scholarly in it. Everything is simple and unified as it is in the Gospel: "it is a spirituality of the Father's love and of a thirst for souls which make up a living memorial to Jesus Christ" (AL, p. 278). This spirituality that Alphonsus proposes to all is the same as the one he proposed to his brothers in his new congregation. He did not ask them to become a new order of preachers, but to be true witnesses of the Gospel, a transparency of Christ. That is why, in his morality—which was first written for them, let us not forget!—if he firmly denounced sin, he called for mercy towards the sinner. For this reason, he was vigorously opposed to the practice of "delay of absolution"—which consisted of imposing, on the penitents, the obligation for them to return to the confessional after a period of several days before they were able to obtain absolution for their sins. Let us listen to Alphonsus's lively reaction to this:

> The more that souls are plunged in vice and under the
> control of the devil, the more we must welcome them
> with tenderness in order to remove them from the claws
> of Satan and put them back into the arms of Jesus Christ.
> Isn't it mean to say: "You are damned, I can't give you
> absolution"? We forget that Jesus Christ also paid the
> price of his blood for this person (SSL, p. 167).

Thus, Alphonsus's preoccupation was not to develop original
moral theories, but to help the confessor to fulfill his ministry to
the poor and the sinners. He wrote: "The office of the confessor
is the greatest: it pledges eternal salvation" (SSL, p. 438).

Wasn't his first concern the same as that of Jesus, the Good
Shepherd, to bring back the sheep who had strayed?

> Certain confessors, proponents of rigidness, only lead souls
> by the pathways of rigorousness. With an excessive abso-
> luteness, they affirm that all of the recidivists will get worse
> and worse if we absolve them before they mend their ways.
> I would like to ask these "masters" who teach this lesson
> to me: do these spurned recidivists, sent away without
> absolution, deprived of the grace of the sacrament, be-
> come stronger and correct themselves of everything? How
> many of these poor, sad people have I encountered who,
> because we have refused them absolution, have fallen into
> despair and lived years of separation detesting the sacra-
> ments (HSE, p. 184).

One day, he was heard to scream: "We know that our modern
directors of souls have no other focus than pushing the faithful
away from the sacraments. It is as if, to go to God, there is no
other path than the one that leads us away from him! I would like
it if these people would themselves have half of the dispositions
that certain confessors require from their penitents, in order to be
worthy to celebrate Mass!" (SSL, p. 29).

The patron of moralists and confessors, Alphonsus wrote a

work that was filled with experience, not a abstract morality. His *Moral Theology* sums up years of confessions celebrated during the parish missions that he preached in numerous dioceses. However, this tireless worker who had made the vow to not lose one minute of his time (a unique case in the history of the saints!) did not omit to do research on this subject for the books he wrote which treated this. Father Louis Gaudé, CSsR, the author of a critique of Alphonsus's *Moral Theology*, could count about 70,000 citations from more than 800 authors. However, his ministry of confession first relies, not on the authority of the moralist writers who preceded him, but on very simple convictions: he asks for a belief in the mercy of the Lord, trust in the good will of the penitent and, above all, the converting power of the sacraments of the Eucharist and reconciliation. This attitude puts him in direct opposition to the Jansenists and the rigorists of his time. Let us hear what he has to say:

> Do not frighten penitents by delaying their absolution from month to month, as is the fashion. This does not help them, but results in their loss. When a sinner acknowledges his sins and despises them, he must not be left alone to fight against temptation. He must be helped, and the best help is the grace of the sacraments.... Do many sinners lack a sufficient disposition for absolution? Then let them be inspired with feelings of repentance by vividly presenting to them the gravity of sin, its offense against God, paradise lost, and hell opening beneath their feet. In this, one sees the charity of the confessor. There are some who would make of sinners so much kindling for the fires of hell! Let them rather give the sinner a helping hand! (LM, pp. 103–4).

This moral theology was something new. It was adopted by the Church in the following century. Many priests were strongly influenced by it. But the most savory fruit of this renewed morality would be Saint John Vianney. In effect, at the beginning of his ministry, the Curé of Ars, a curate for fourteen years, felt obligated in conscience to defer many absolutions. Because of this, his penitents who came from afar made a fortune for the innkeepers of Ars, Trévoux, and Lyons, while waiting days and weeks for a pardon from God and the Church. But the bishop of Belley, Monsignor Devie, a fervent Liguorian, recommended Thomas-Marie-Joseph Gousset's 1829 work, *The Justification for the Moralism of Liguori*. For Vianney, this shook up his ministry of penitence. Gone were the delays for absolution. Gone also was the extra profit for the innkeepers of the region. He came to say: "Truly, how could I be so harsh on these people who have come from so far away, who have made so many sacrifices and who are so often obligated to hide in order to come here?" (HSE, p. 186).

At the source of this moral theology, there was the faith in the mercy of God towards sinners and respect for the conscience of the sinner. In fact, Alphonsus only followed Saint Paul when he affirmed: "...for whatever does not proceed from faith is sin" (Rom 14:23). Furthermore, all of Saint Alphonsus's spirituality is characterized by a firm sense of hope, echoing the conviction of the Apostle (see 1 Tim 2:4). Did he not say, "God wants all of us to be saved; eternal damnation is saved for the stubborn and them alone" (SSL, p. 330)?

In fact, for Alphonsus, Christ is mankind's hope, and primarily the hope for sinners and the poor. He is hope because he made himself become a man. He is hope because he made himself become incarnate into a world of poor people, because he worked like a poor person among the poor. He is hope because, throughout his entire public life, he revealed to everyone (without distinction for race, nationality, class, culture, or sex) that they were, all of them, children of the same father. He is hope because he came to free mankind from sin and all of its consequences. And he freed them through his death and resurrection by giving his life like a poor person and by giving us his risen life like only a poor God, God of love, could give. For all of that, Christ is truly the hope of all mankind, with priority given to the poor.

If Alphonsus has been proclaimed by the Church as the pa-

tron for confessors and moralists, it is because he was a witness
for hope in the mercy of the Lord. A witness of this hope, he lived
the priesthood, religious life, and the episcopate in a different way
than many of the people of his time. He proposes his ideal, to
love God by loving the poor, to us today just as he proposed it to
his young novices in 1749:

> Whoever is called to the Congregation of the Most Holy
> Redeemer will never be a true "continuer" of Jesus Christ
> and will never become a saint if he doesn't seek the goal
> of his vocation and doesn't have the spirit of the institute,
> which is to save souls, those who are the most deprived
> of spiritual support, like the poor people of the country-
> side (Consideration XIII for those who are called to the
> religious vocation).

AND US, TODAY?

Are we, like Alphonsus and his companions, witnesses for hope
and mercy of the Lord Jesus, who showed so much love for all
mankind and especially for the poor?

Faced with numerous personal or collective moral problems
in our time (from abortion to euthanasia, from bioethics to international finances, from racial violence to nuclear armaments, and
so on), are we concerned to honestly analyze the situations and
trust in the good will of the people who seek to act in a moral
way? Do we make the effort to clear our conscience and to respect that of others? Is our morality legalistic or rigorous, or one
of conscience, love, mercy, and freedom like that of Saint
Alphonsus, following the Gospel which invites us to discover it,
to support our actions?

Finally, when faced with extraordinary spiritual phenomena
(visions, prophecies, messages, stigmata, healings, and so on), do
we elect, like Saint Alphonsus and the Church of today, to remain humble and discreet, convinced that what is essential is elsewhere?

My eternal God…what hope of pardon would there be
for me if you had not given me Jesus Christ
so that he might be the hope of us miserable sinners?
"He is the atoning sacrifice for our sins" (1 Jn 2:2).
Yes, by sacrificing his life in satisfaction for
the wrongs we have done you, he has given you more
honor than we have dishonor by our sins.
Receive me, therefore, O my Father,
through the love of Jesus Christ.
I repent, O Infinite Goodness,
for having outraged you….
Receive an ungrateful child, who had once forsaken
you but who returns to you today,
with a firm resolution to love you.
Yes, my Father, I love you,
and will always love you.
O my beloved Father, now that I know the love
you have given me,
and the patience you have shown me,
I don't know how to live without loving you….
O Mary, God is my Father, and you are my Mother.
You can do all things with God; help me;
obtain for me holy perseverance and his holy love.
Amen (N, pp. 24–25).

REFLECTION QUESTIONS

Do I desire a union with God that is full and complete? Do I recognize that Jesus Christ saved me by his Incarnation, his death on the cross, and his Resurrection? I am saved and I am called to participate in this salvation by giving my life over to Jesus and the Good News he proclaimed. I am called to live in the spirit, not in the law. How well does the life I am currently living respond to this call?

DAY EIGHT

The Lord Loves You, Love Him Back!

FOCUS POINT

God loves us immensely, this is clear. He sent his Son to us to let us know just how much he loves us. God loved us into creation, graces us with the desire to pray to him, to love him, and to serve him by serving the people (family, friends, strangers) he has graced us to know in our lives. We are called to respond to God with our own love—a love that is put into action.

During a trip to Italy, on the occasion of the two hundred and fiftieth anniversary of the foundation of the Congregation of the Most Holy Redeemer, on the program, there was a visit to the General Archives of the Redemptorists in Rome. One of the most moving moments was the one in which we were allowed to see, open, and touch the little pocket booklet of eighty-eight pages (bound in parchment) that Saint Alphonsus always carried with him,

which he entitled, *Cose di Coscienza*, "Matters of Conscience."
On page thirty-six, we could read the following: "Jesus loves me,
I follow in his sorrowful footsteps; he made me know this so I
would be more aware.... The Virgin Mary loves me as one of her
most beloved sons...Jesus entrusted me to her, so that she may
accompany me in the conversion of souls...."

"Jesus loves me, Mary loves me"—the secret of Saint
Alphonsus's spirituality lies in these two loves, Jesus and Mary.
Isn't his spirituality primarily differentiated by faith in the infinite tenderness of the Lord and confidence in the maternal intercession by Mary? In the century of Jansenism and the most severe
rigorism, Alphonsus's meditation on the paschal mystery of the
salvation of humanity which was lived by Jesus and continued by
his apostles, led him to discover that our salvation is a work of
love, a gift from God and not a reward for our merits:

> Indeed, what two great mysteries of hope and love we
> have in the Passion of Jesus Christ and the sacrament of
> the altar! These two mysteries should inflame with love
> and reduce to ashes all of our hearts. And what sinners
> are there, be they ever so dissolute, who could despair of
> pardon if they repent of the evil they have done, when
> they see a God so in love with human beings and so in-
> clined to do them good? (AA, p. 26).

Alphonsus never stopped preaching or speaking about this Good
News that God loves us. We find it echoed in his *Meditations on
the Incarnation*: "Is it true, yes or no? Nevertheless—and this is
sad enough to make you cry—does all mankind let him touch them?
Are all inclined to reply with the same love?" (SSL, p. 156–7).

We think that we are hearing Francis of Assisi running in the
streets of the city, moaning: "Love is not loved! Love is not loved!"
For Alphonsus, mankind can only find its happiness, its true happiness, a happiness that is of the same level as that of God, by
responding to this divine love with love in return. Alphonsus shares
this conviction with his readers in one of his most famous works,

The Practice of the Love of Jesus Christ. Published in 1768, this masterpiece went all over the world. Alphonsus begins with the apostle Paul's call: "...just as the Lord has forgiven you, so you also must forgive. Above all, clothe yourself with love, which binds everything together in perfect harmony" (Col 3:13, 14), then comments on the hymn to charity (love) in the thirteenth chapter of the First Letter to the Corinthians:

> Jesus Christ, by the sole fact that he is God, merits all our love. But, through the proof of the love he has given us, he wanted to put us in a kind of state of necessity to love him, at least for certain benefits and suffering. He loved us a great deal so that we would love him a great deal... (AA, p. 57).

Alphonsus was a lover, a lover of God. He always had the verb "to love" on his lips. However, this love for God is a response to a love that came before it—a response that commits him to an adventure of love; a love that is fed, not only with feelings, but with many actions; and, primarily, the action of leaving everything, of detaching oneself from everything to be able to welcome the immense love of God. In the same way as Saint Teresa of Ávila (his "spiritual mother," one could say), Alphonsus wrote the following in one of his *Letters*:

> To love God completely brings two things along with it: the first is to break all attachments that are not for God or according to God...the second is the prayer by which the holy love invades the heart. But if the heart does not empty itself of earthly things, the love cannot enter it, for there is no room. Conversely, a heart that is detached from all creatures soon inflames itself with the fire of a divine love that grows with each breath of grace (SSL, p. 343).

This love is demanding, but it is available to everyone. In his preaching, as in a booklet he published in 1754, *On Conversing Continually and Familiarly With God*, Alphonsus repeated it often:

> God loves you! Love him.... He is always close to you... inside you.... In the morning, he is there to spoon words of affection or trust into your lips, in order to receive...the offering of your day: acts of virtue and good works to which you promise to use to please him, pains that you declare to willingly suffer for his glory and love (HSE, p. 198).

This love is available to everyone on the condition that it is requested in a humble prayer. That is why Alphonsus never stopped praying and calling to the Spirit, to love with a Pentecostal love:

> *O divine Spirit, I no longer want to live just for myself;*
> *I want to use the remainder of my life to love you,*
> *to please you.*
> *Also, I beg for you to grant me the gift of prayer;*
> *come into my heart; teach me, yourself,*
> *how to do it well.*
> *Give me the necessary energy so I won't neglect it*
> *in disgust, in moments of spiritual aridity.*
> *Give me a spirit of prayer, I mean the grace to*
> *always pray and address the requests that are*
> *the most agreeable to your divine Heart.*
> *My sins have already caused me to be lost;*
> *but the many indications of your tenderness make me*
> *see that you want my salvation and sanctification;*
> *Well! Yes, I want to sanctify myself in order to please*
> *you and love your infinite bounty even more.*
> *I love you, O my Sovereign Good, my Love,*
> *my Everything! Because I love you,*
> *I give myself completely to you.*
> *O Mary, my Hope, protect me. Amen (VS, p. 310).*

AND US, TODAY?

The fundamental characteristic of the spirituality of Saint Alphonsus is that it is a *spirituality of love*, of a burning love. Alphonsus was a saint of fire, a saint of the Pentecost. He passionately loved Jesus and Mary. From them, he learned true love. He responds to it, he still gives witness today by the way he lived his life, and through his words and his writings.

And us? Are we the kind of Christian who takes the time to let ourselves be loved by God, to let ourselves be inflamed by this love of the risen One?

Are we Christians of fire, or Christians who have been extinguished? Are we Christians of the Pentecost, which our world needs so much today? And this fire of love, when it burns in our veins, do we care to tell others about it?

What do we do to better know and love the Lord even more? Are we the kind of Christians who love the people of today, Christians who are open to this modern world where Jesus is already present, where he came before us and where he awaits us?

Do we recognize the values brought by this modernism? Do we also reject the false values seen here, and help this world of modern men and women convert themselves so they can receive happiness that is eternal and universal?

O my beloved Redeemer,
if I could only have all of mankind's hearts in my
possession so I could love you with all of these united
hearts as much you deserve to be loved!
Why is it, that on this earth,
where you shed all of your blood,
O God of Love, and given your life for the love of man,
why, I ask myself, is it that so few burn with love for you?
You came down from heaven to inject the fire
of this love into our hearts,
you ardently wanted to see it kindled:
"I came to bring fire to the earth,
and how I wish it were already kindled!" (Lk 12:49).

Thus, I pray, with the holy Church, to set my heart,
and all the hearts of mankind, afire with your love:
Tui amoris in eis ignem accende, accende, accende!
O God, all goodness, all love! O infinite lovability!
O Infinite Love! Make yourself known to us,
make us all love you.
Knowing that, up until now, I, more than others,
have scorned your love, I am not ashamed to address
this prayer to you, because now,
illuminated with your enlightenment and wounded
with so many arrows of love that you have shot from
your heart which is burning with tenderness for my soul,
I no longer want to persist in my former ingratitude;
but I want to love you with all of my strength,
I want to be an intense flame of love for you;
you must grant me this grace.
I seek neither the consolation
nor the tenderness of your love;
I am not worthy and I do not ask them of you:
to love you is enough for me. Yes, I love you,
O my Sovereign Good!
I love you, my God, my Everything:
Deus meus, et omnia! Amen (VS, p. 454).

REFLECTION QUESTIONS

Do I pray for the strength to love God—to respond to his love—
with all that I have, with all that I am? Do I seek to strip from my
life all the attachments that prevent me from loving God as I
should? Do I pray that God will invade my heart, and ignite within
me the passion to love without concern for anyone, even those
the world considers not worthy of love? How does Mary's love
for her son Jesus (and for me) inspire me to love God and others?

DAY NINE

From the Starry Heavens

FOCUS POINT

Alphonsus sought to bring the Good News to the poor, and the poor to the Good News. Alphonsus had a different approach with the poor than he had with intellectuals. With intellectuals, Alphonsus employed intellectual arguments, some theologically complex. With the poor, though, Saint Alphonsus turned the focus to the beauty of the child Jesus as he lay in the manger. To look upon the face of the child who is God is to know love and to love God.

S aint Alphonsus Liguori was the Saint of the Century of Enlightenment. His knowledge was quite broad: he knew literature, mathematics, physics, astronomy, and philosophy, not to forget the fine arts. He wrote poems and was a talented artist. But in music, he was "in the same class as a renowned master," having composed certain pieces which have been played in major world centers, made into records, and used in films. One of his most celebrated Christmas pieces, written in 1755, *Tu scendi dalle stelle, O Re del Cielo* ("You Come Down From the Stars, O King of Heaven"), goes as follows:

> *From the starry heavens,*
> *You descend, O Lord,*
> *From the cold, the ice,*
> *You come to withstand the harshness.*

Giuseppi Verdi, the celebrated composer, in 1890, said: "Without this song by Alphonsus, Christmas isn't Christmas." Alphonsus certainly sings of the Christmas mystery, but he primarily invites the Christian people to enter into that mystery:

> Many Christians have the habit, in their homes, of preparing, well in advance, a manger to represent the birth of Christ; but, alas, how few are the number of them who think to prepare, in their hearts, a suitable dwelling, where Jesus Christ can be born and rest! Let us be like these people... (N, p. 25).

Alphonsus had meditated on the mystery of the child Jesus for a long time and put this meditation into writing. When he had his book, *Meditations on the Incarnation*, published in 1758, he developed his favorite themes into ten discourses: "The eternal Word, from God, he made himself a man; from greatness made small; from a master, a servant; from innocent, guilty; from powerful, weak; from everything for himself, to everything for everyone; from blessed, suffering; from rich, poor; from very exalted, humbled" (SSL, p. 108).

For Alphonsus, to meditate on the mystery of Christmas was very important, for it was the revelation of the true face of God, this unexpected God who first appeared as a small Jewish baby. This God, burning with love for us, came to light the fire of his love in the hearts of all mankind, in order to inflame them with love for him and for their brothers and sisters on earth. Let us listen to the beginning of the first of Alphonsus's discourses for the novena of Christmas:

> The Jews celebrated a feast day they called *dies ignis*, the day of fire, "in order that you also may celebrate...the festival of the fire given when Nehemiah, who built the temple and the altar, offered sacrifices" (2 Macc 1:18) upon his return with his countrymen from the captivity of Babylon. It is thus, and indeed with more reason, that Christmas day should be called the day of fire, when God came as a little child to kindle the fire of love in the hearts of mankind. "I came to kindle fire on the earth," said Jesus Christ; his wish was realized. Before the coming of the Messiah, who loved God upon earth? Hardly was he known in the small corner of the world known as Judea; and even there, how very few loved him when he came! As to the rest of the world, some worshiped the sun, some animals, some statues made of stone, and others again even more vile creatures still. But after the coming of Jesus Christ, the name of God was preached across the entire universe, and he was loved by many souls: God was more loved by mankind in a few years than he had been in the previous four thousand years, since the creation of man (N, pp. 126–7).

His Tenth Discourse caused him a few problems with the court of Naples. Had he not dared to write about the manger in Bethlehem:

> Let us arise and enter, the door is open; "there are no guards," said Saint Peter Chrysologus, "to say that this is not the time." Monarchs shut themselves up in their palaces, and these palaces are surrounded with soldiers: it is not easy to have an audience with princes; those who would speak to them must expect to have their patience tried; they will often be sent away and told to come again—that this is not the time for an audience. It is com-

pletely different with Jesus Christ: he remains in that manger, and he is there as a little child, attracting all who come to see him; and the manger is open, without guards and without doors; so that all may go in when they please to see this small little King, speak to him, and even to embrace him, if they love him and desire him.

Let every soul, then, enter! Behold and see that tender Infant, who is weeping as he lies in the manger on that miserable straw. See how beautiful he is; look at the light which he sends forth, and the love which he inspires; those eyes send out arrows of fire to the hearts that desire him: his cries are flames for his true friends, "the very stable, the very straw cry out," says Saint Bernard, "to tell you to love the one who loves you so much" (N, p. 225).

Alphonsus's originality was to start to examine the mystery of Christmas by referring to, not learned reflections or easy sentiments, but simply to the most common human experience: "All children soften the hearts of those who see them with love. Who then would not love God with all of his tenderness when he discovers him as a small baby, needing to be fed, shivering in the cold, poor, reduced to nothing, abandoned, who cries, who wails in a manger, on the straw."

No detail left him indifferent: everything brought his admiration and recognition. But his contemplation of the mystery of Christmas elicits the most burning emotions from him: "I love you, O my very little Savior; I love you, my child God; I love you, O my love, my life, my everything!"

Here, Alphonsus's spirituality appears like a spirituality of the Incarnation: it is rooted in the Gospel of the childhood of Jesus and in the popular piety. Alphonsus welcomes this devotion and evangelizes it. He never sought to lure the elite intellectuals. He wanted to nourish and affirm the faith of all Christian people, including the little ones. And he was successful: the vast diffusion of his writings give testimony to it.

AND US, TODAY?

What place do we give to the contemplation of the mystery of the Incarnation of the Word? Saint Alphonsus, nourished by the texts of the Fathers of the Church, gave them great importance. In fact, this contemplation of the doctrine of the edification of the Christian is very well explained by Saint Irenaeus of Lyons: "God made himself become a man so that man could become God."

And us? Do we scorn the popular devotions who plunge their roots into this incredible mystery of Christmas? Or, do we care to discern the riches there in order to nourish and prolong our liturgical life with it?

Are we preoccupied, not only with nourishing our faith through the contemplation of Christmas, but also, like Saint Alphonsus, to build our "interior manger," where we could welcome, serve, and love our Savior? And with him, our brothers and sisters on earth?

Dear Infant, I see you in the manger already nailed to
the cross which is constantly present for you
and you have already accepted for me.
O my crucified Infant,
I thank you for it and I love you.
Stretched out on this straw,
you are already suffering for me, and even now,
are preparing yourself to die because of your love for
me, you command and invite me to love you:
"You shall love the Lord your God with all your
heart..." (Deut 6:5; Mt 22:37).
And I want nothing more than to love you.
Since you willed that I should love you,
give me all the love that you require of me.
Our love for you is your gift,
the greatest gift you can make to a soul.
Accept, O my Jesus, for your lover a sinner
who has so greatly offended you.
You came from heaven to seek the lost sheep.

You seek me, therefore, I will seek only you.
You want my soul,
and my soul wants nothing else but you.
You said: "I love those who love me…" (Prov 8:17).
I love you, love me as well; and if you love me,
bind me to your love so tightly that I may never be
able to untie myself from you.
Mary, my Mother, help me. Let it be your glory
also to see your son loved by a miserable sinner,
who has, until this time, so greatly offended him.
Amen (N, pp. 32–3).

REFLECTION QUESTIONS

Do I often contemplate the mystery of the Incarnation? Christmas offers me this opportunity; do I nourish my faith by praying before a manger scene, dwelling on the beauty and simplicity of the child Jesus in his crib? Do I clear a space in the manger of my heart so that Jesus will have a place to dwell and rest? Am I able to keep the Incarnation in mind and heart all throughout the year? How can contemplation of the Incarnation become a part of my regular spiritual life?

DAY TEN

My Jesus,
Everything Is for You

FOCUS POINT

Alphonsus meditated often on the Passion of Jesus, and preached on it, as well. The Passion of our Lord had everything to do with his great and abiding love for each one of us. This love was given to us so that God and mankind would no longer be separated by sin. Jesus gave us everything he had—his love, his caring, his suffering, and finally his life. How else can we respond to this love except to return our own love to God as best we can?

─────

If we visit the Redemptorist house in Pagani, we can see, on the second floor, next to the oratory, the small room where Saint Alphonsus worked towards the end of his life. On the bleached wooden table we can see a holy image of Our Lady of Good Counsel and a crucifix. Alphonsus wrote the words, "My Jesus, everything is for you," at the foot of it in his blood. Diligent for meditating upon the mystery of the Passion of Jesus, he made it a rule for his companions and published ten or so volumes or booklets on this favorite theme. Endlessly, this meditation elicited cries of admiration and love from him:

> Yes, my gentle Redeemer, let me say it, you are crazy with love! Is it not foolish for you to have wanted to die for me, for a worm, an ungrateful person, a sinner, and a traitor? But if you, my God, have become crazy with love for me, how could I not become crazy with love for you? After having seen you die for me, how could I think anything else of you? How could I love anything other than you?
>
> O whips, O thorns, O nails, O crosses, O wounds, O agonies, O death of Jesus, you push me too much, you force me too much to love the one who loved me so much. O incarnate Word, O loving God, my soul is enamored with you; I want to love you to the point of no longer finding any pleasure in anything other than giving you pleasure, O my very dear Lord! (HSE, p. 173).

If you continue your trip beyond Pagani all the way to Ciorani, they will not forget to show you, in the Redemptorist convent there, the canvas of Jesus, dead on the cross that was painted by Alphonsus at the age of twenty-three, when he was a young lawyer. Later, having become a priest, he had it reproduced on cards and life-size likenesses which were exhibited at the end of a mission. This canvas is the translation, in paint, of the shock that Alphonsus received on a certain day in 1719 when he was contemplating the crucified Jesus. It is repeated in the following lines from his book, *The Way of Salvation*:

> My soul, lift your eyes, and contemplate this crucified Christ; contemplate the divine Lamb sacrificed on the altar of his sacrifice. Reflect on the fact that he is the beloved Son of the eternal Father, and that he died through

love for you. Look at his arms, extended to welcome you, his head inclined to give you the kiss of peace, his side open to receive you into his heart. What do you have to say before this God who is so loving? Does he deserve to be loved? Listen to what he had to suggest right from up on the cross: "Examine, my child, if there is anyone in the world who has a greater love for you than I do" (VS, p. 292).

When he published his book, *Meditations on the Passion of Jesus Christ*, Alphonsus had the above mentioned image of Jesus engraved on the cover of his book, adding some arrows which flowed from his five open wounds. Alphonsus was not primarily interested in Jesus' physical suffering, but in the revelation of his love for us—the fact that he suffered for us. He expressly stated it in the first chapter of his book, *The Practice of the Love of Jesus Christ*:

> "For the love of Christ urges us on" (2 Cor 5:14). What did the apostle Paul mean? He meant that it is not so much the sufferings of Jesus Christ, as the love he showed us in enduring them that obliges, and all but constrains us to love him (AA, p. 5).

In short, for Alphonsus, the Word made flesh did not come onto the earth in order to break records for physical suffering in terms of endurance or in intensity! He came to tell us and to show us his love. These arrows which leave from Christ's wounds have no other significance:

> But what could have ever led a God to die, executed on a cross between two villains—such a disgrace to his divine majesty? "Who did this?" asks Saint Bernard. "It was love," he answers, "which knows no dignity." See how love, when it wants to make itself known, doesn't go looking for what best befits the dignity of the lover, but what

will serve best to show itself to the beloved. So Saint
Francis of Paola had very good reason to cry out, at the
sight of a crucifix, "O love, O love, O love!" Likewise,
when we look at Jesus on the cross, we should cry out
those very same words (AA, p. 6).

Each day as well as several times a day throughout his entire
adult life, Alphonsus meditated upon the Passion of Jesus. And
he invited people to contemplate the crucified Christ, for his meditation of the Passion is not a morbid meditation on the sufferings
and the death of Jesus, but a wondrous contemplation on the
love of God for mankind that was revealed at that time: "No one
has greater love than this, to lay down one's life for one's friends"
(Jn 15:13).

Such is an indication of the spirituality of Alphonsus: it is a
spirituality of the Passion, in the sense of the love of the Son of
God for all mankind revealed on the cross and in his death—the
resurrection of Jesus who gave his life and who gives us the Life.
Alphonsus calls us to discover this love, and respond to it, to live
it and to be witnesses of it. That is what he wrote, what he
preached, and what he continuously lived.

For Alphonsus, the crucified Christ was Christ in his mystery
of love. Love was always first: "God's love was revealed among
us in this way: God sent his only Son into the world so that we
might live through him. In this is love, not that we loved God but
that he loved us and sent his Son to be the atoning sacrifice for
our sins" (1 Jn 4:9–10).

This love, so well brought forth by the apostle John, deserves
our love. To respond to this love with a true love is all holiness in
the eyes of Alphonsus. This true love for Christ draws its strength
in the contemplation of the crucified Christ, the death of Christ,
the summit of his love for mankind. That is why Alphonsus demanded the members of his congregation meditate upon the Passion of Jesus and preach it:

The conversions that come through fear don't last very long, we shrug our shoulders and they're gone.... But if we are converted through the love of the crucified Jesus, the conversion is stronger and more durable. Fear can't do what isn't done through love. And when we attach ourselves to the crucified Christ, we have no more fear (SSL, pp. 466–7).

AND US, TODAY?

For Alphonsus, the cross was the path to the discovery of the Lord's love and a sign of victory: did it not indicate the time when the glorified Christ glorified his disciples? In other words, his spirituality of the cross is a paschal spirituality.

Is our contemplation of the Passion of the Savior similar to that of Alphonsus? Are we content to let ourselves be moved by the sufferings of the crucified Christ, or have we taken the time to discover the deeper meaning: God loves us, God loves me, do I love him?

The love of the crucified Christ upset Alphonsus's heart, does it upset ours?

Jesus asked his disciples to follow him on this path of love: that path always passes by the cross. Did he not say, "If any want to become my followers, let them deny themselves and take up their cross and follow me" (Mk 8:34)? Are we following this road?

Furthermore, do we know how to recognize the crucified Christ today? "Lord, when was it that we saw you hungry or thirsty or a stranger or naked or sick or in prison..." (Mt 25:44).

Through the dramatic daily events of today's world, do we know how to recognize the limitless numbers of Stations of the Cross where the crucified Christ, today just as before, "is in agony until the end of the world"?

Was it possible that God, the creator of all things,
would have been pleased to die for
the love of his creatures?

Yes, it is through faith that he has done so.
"As Christ loved us and gave himself up for us…"
(Eph 5:2). The earth, the heavens, and all nature,
with astonishment, witnessed Jesus,
the only begotten Son of God,
the Lord of the universe,
die in intense pain and anguish, like a criminal,
on a disgraceful cross. Why? For the love of mankind.
And are there those amongst them who believe
in this love that Jesus Christ has for them and
not love him back?
Lord, I am one of these people,
I have known your Passion and
not only have I not loved you,
but I have frequently offended you.
Pardon me, I beg you, and remind me continually of
the death which you have suffered through love for me,
so that I may never again offend you,
but may always love you….
My crucified Jesus, I want to be yours alone,
now and forever, and I will love no one else but you.
Strengthen my weakness and make me
forever faithful to you.
Mary, my Mother, help me to love Jesus;
this is the only favor I ask of you.
Amen (VS, pp. 96–7).

REFLECTION QUESTIONS

Do I often contemplate the Passion of the crucified Christ? When I do, what do I feel? Am I overcome with sadness, gratitude, or some other emotion? How do I respond to the great love shown me by Christ on the cross? Do I unite my own suffering with that of Jesus during times of sickness or pain? When I do this, do I recognize the unity that suffering can provide between the God who loves me and the God I love?

DAY ELEVEN

Blessed Flowers

FOCUS POINT

As a lawyer, Alphonsus decorated the altar of his parish church with flowers. This devotion continued throughout his life, as he decorated tabernacles with various flowers and vegetation. Alphonsus visited the risen Christ in the Eucharist, in the tabernacle, to contemplate the presence of Jesus Christ and his love for us. Alphonsus encouraged perpetual adoration of the Blessed Sacrament throughout his life, inviting people to become like flowers and decorate the tabernacle with their presence and devotion.

During Holy Week of 1722, in the course of a closed retreat with the Lazarists, Saint Alphonsus had the experience, like Saint Paul, that "Christ Jesus has made me his own" (Phil 3:12). Alphonsus's biographer, Tannoia, reminds us that it was a time when he visited the Blessed Sacrament every day, "at the church which exposed it for the forty hour period, in whatever city or town he was in that day, no matter how far he was from home...."

It delayed him for hours...he was beautiful to see, often in his dress habit, courting the divine Host of the altars" (SSL, p. 114). It was not the solemn ceremony with incense, candles, and Gregorian chants in honor of the Blessed Sacrament that drew him, but the loving visit, the prolonged, contemplative, and loving adoration of the one who died and rose for mankind, and who offered his life and his love to allow each person to live of this life and to love this offered love. Alphonsus wrote in one of his *Visits to the Blessed Sacrament*: "It was good to stay at the foot of the altar and speak in a familiar way with the eucharistic Jesus, to ask him for his love and bountiful graces!" (HSE, p. 60).

Like all of the lovers of the world, Alphonsus spoke of his love with flowers. Previously, as a young lawyer, he decorated the altar of his parish church with flowers. Throughout his entire life, as his biographer tells us, he continued "to decorate his beloved of the tabernacle with all varieties of meridional (southern) flowers and vegetation." In the convents where he lived, he procured the most rare seeds, then went to pick the flowers with his own hands to decorate the altar. He envied the happiness of these innocent creatures because they could stay, day and night, next to their Creator. He expressed this in the following way in his *Hymns and Verses*:

> *Blessed flowers, which, day and night,*
> *Always remain close to Jesus,*
> *Sure to shine, in order to wither, around*
> *This God of love!*
> *How I wish I could also arrange my stay*
> *Next to the Life, to be from his garden!*
> *I envy your place in life: (to have) my turn to live there,*
> *To die there of love (SSL, p. 114–5).*

He not only took the time to visit the risen Christ in his Eucharist, but he also took the time to preach about the Eucharist and write about it. First, he wrote a few pages to nourish the prayers of his young novices at Ciorani. One day, a layperson (who was converted by him), who was making a retreat in this community, heard the texts of one of his *Visits* read. Enthusiastic, he wanted to pay, himself, to have them printed for the use of the general public. But there were only fifteen. He asked Alphonsus to write fifteen more so that there would be one for each day of the month. This was done and the work was published in 1745. And it was a resounding success! Today, there are more than two thousand editions in about forty languages! His biographer does not hesitate to write: "We could affirm, without fear of error, that the European eucharistic awakening in the second half of the eighteenth century and all of the nineteenth was due to this little booklet, a true example of Alphonsus's piety and of the most authentic Catholic devotion" (HSE, p. 174).

Had he not encouraged frequent Communion, in opposition to the restrictions that many priests brought, at that time, to the reception of the sacraments:

> Someone might say: "But this is why I can't go to Communion more often, because I am so cold in my love of God." Jean de Gerson answers this sort of person: "So, because you feel cold, do you move away from the fire?" Since you feel cold, you should approach this sacrament all the more frequently, so long as you wish to love Jesus Christ. Saint Bonaventure writes: "Even though you feel lukewarm, approach anyway, take Communion and trust in the mercy of God. The sicker you feel, the more you need the doctor." In a similar vein, Saint Francis de Sales writes: "Two sorts of persons ought to take frequent Communion: the perfect, in order to stay that way; and the imperfect, in order to reach perfection" (AA, p. 20).

Few Christian writers have spoken with such fervor for the Eucharist. He popularized *Visits to the Blessed Sacrament and to the Blessed Virgin*, and encouraged perpetual adoration, day and night in some churches, as it is still done today in the Sacred Heart of Montmartre Basilica in Paris.

Daily eucharistic meetings characterize Saint Alphonsus's spirituality. For him, as it was later for Charles de Foucauld, it is the sacrament of love and life: with the risen Jesus, he gains the strength to love and live by drawing from the source of all living water.

> The source of every good, Jesus in the most holy Sacrament, says: "let anyone who is thirsty come to me" (Jn 7:37)...for there, Jesus dispenses all the merits of his Passion...what do I do in the presence of the Blessed Sacrament? Why am I not asked, instead, what is not done there? We love, we ask, we praise, we give thanks. We ask, what does a poor man do in the presence of one who is rich? What does a sick man do in the presence of his physician? What does a man do who is parched with thirst in the presence of a clear fountain? What is the occupation of one who is starving, and is placed before a splendid table? (VSS, p. 127–8).

The spirituality of Alphonsus is a eucharistic spirituality. At a time when so many people go to the ends of the earth to seek the true religion, the true face of God, or techniques to discover it, Alphonsus invites us, with flowers, with texts, with his own example, to contemplate the love of the risen Lord present among us, close to us, the source of love, the source of life. Let us understand it well: what is important is not necessarily to use the same methods and the same formula which date back to the eighteenth century, but to let Saint Alphonsus communicate to us the fire of his love for the eucharistic Jesus and open the path to the upper room for us, the path of loving and warm prayer. And for us, then, to pursue it in our own way.... The layperson who was converted by Alphonsus, who was the impetus behind Alphonsus's *Visits to the Blessed Sacrament*, did not make a mistake. These *Visits* are a school for prayer.

AND US, TODAY?

In his era, Alphonsus was the man of the liturgical renewal requested by the Council of Trent. He participated completely in this renewal. With this in mind, in 1760, he even wrote a small booklet called *The Mass and Office Hurriedly Said*, in order to promote celebrations of quality.

And us? What is our own participation in the liturgical renewal that has been requested by Vatican Council II? Furthermore, where are we with respect to this discovery of the loving proximity of God? Is the Eucharist the source of our strength to love?

Have we truly understood that the Eucharist is not only the sacrament of the "real presence" of the Lord, but also the sacrament of the "real communion" with the Lord? We take and eat the body of Christ in order to be purified, reconciled, gathered, and "Christified," to be better able to fulfill our mission in the world. In other words, the Eucharist is the paschal sacrament of our transformation and of that of the world: are we conscious of this?

In effect, is the Eucharist not the place where the Holy Spirit, like in the upper room, gathers us together through faith to send us out to our brothers and sisters in order to proclaim the love of the Father and gather all mankind together?

My beloved Jesus,
O God so overflowing with love for mankind,
what more could you invent to make yourself
more loved by the ungrateful?
Oh, if all mankind loved you, we would always see a
multitude of people hurrying into churches, prostrated,
face down on the floor in order to adore and thank you,
transported by love for the One whose eyes of faith
they see hidden in the tabernacle.
But no, mankind forgets you; you and your love.
They leave you there, O my God, alone,
without any company,

to run after a man from whom they hope
to gain a few miserable favors.
Oh, if I could only repair such ingratitude
with my homages!
How deeply I am distressed
to have gathered them elsewhere,
to have not given witness—
I have also been indifferent and scornful!
But I want to change, and from now on,
to come into your presence most often and for the
longest time that I can.
Inflame me with your love so that I live only to love
you and give you pleasure.
You deserve the love of all of the hearts.
If there was a time when I scorned you,
I now have only one desire: to love you.
My Jesus, you are my love and all my goodness.
Deus meus, et omnia: *My God, my Everything.*
Blessed Virgin Mary, help me gain a great love
for the Blessed Sacrament.
Amen (VS, pp. 323–4).

REFLECTION QUESTIONS

Do I visit the Blessed Sacrament on a regular basis? Is there a regular "holy hour" offered by my local church that I might attend to aid my eucharistic spirituality? Do I recognize the true presence of Jesus Christ in holy Communion? Do I see the Eucharist as the means to experience true "communion" with God? How does this communion with God affect my relationship with others? Does *communion* mean "unity" to me?

DAY TWELVE

Whoever Prays, Saves Himself

FOCUS POINT

Alphonsus was a man of prayer. He stressed perseverance in prayer, both individual and community prayer. Praying with the words of the Gospel was very important to Saint Alphonsus, as was praying the rosary. For Saint Alphonsus, prayer was a necessity, a necessity in the participation in the salvation brought to us through Jesus Christ. The communication that comes with prayer helps us to keep our hearts open to the Word of God and its saving grace.

When numerous Redemptorists from France went on a pilgrimage to "Alphonsian" places in 1982, a surprise awaited them in Pagani. In the morning, one of them called out: "Come, see!" Many of them came out into the street. There, in front of the San Alfonso Basilica, there was a group of young boys and girls walking to their school. The majority of them made a side trip through the porch of the church, stopping for a few minutes; standing at the threshold of the nave, they prayed, then they left to join their class again. This prayer by the young people of Pagani was a tradition that goes back to Saint Alphonsus Liguori! Had he not often meditated on and preached the call of the Lord in this church: "the need to pray always and not to lose heart" (Lk 18:1)?

Alphonsus prayed a great deal. He prayed well. He is called the Doctor of Prayer. He had learned to pray on his mother's lap and in his father's arms. The latter loved to pray, when he was at sea, before the statues of the Passion that he had installed in his commander's cabin: these are preserved today in the Redemptorist museum in Pagani. Alphonsus, who was a great worker his entire life, dedicated many hours each day to prayer. Through experience, he knew that one could only know God and themselves through taking the time for reflection and prayer. This is why he gave so much importance to prayer. He spoke about it often. He invited the faithful to it. He gave advice that was inspired by his own experience, as in this letter to a religious sister dated August 26, 1734:

> I want you to dedicate a full hour to prayer...choose the best time for this, above all the night and the times of great solitude: that is when Jesus speaks to his friends (SSL, p. 299).

Nevertheless, he insisted upon perseverance in prayer and on the quality of the prayer:

> O God of my heart...I know that you always come to help me when I pray to you. But this is my fear: I am afraid to forget to ask for your help and, through my own fault, to have the immense sadness to have lost your grace. Oh, through Jesus Christ's merits, give me the grace of prayer, but the abundant grace to always pray and to pray well.
>
> O Mary, my Mother, give me, through the love that

you have for Jesus Christ, the favor that I ask of you: the one to pray, and to never stop praying until death. Amen (HSE, p. 194–5).

Alphonsus's prayer was not purely an individual prayer, it was turned towards others. It was a plural prayer, community oriented, missionary. He wrote that the true missionary must preach "with his knees" to convert the people for whom he is responsible. He reminds us in one of his *Letters*:

> What is the advantage for the listeners if we just continue to convince them of Christian truths? It consists, above all, of getting them to change their lives and give themselves to God. Thus, whether the preacher of the mission is wary of imitating those who, once the sermon is over, begin to scream: "demand pardon from God! Implore mercy!" or who, by seizing the crucifix, or the bell chords, or torches, is satisfied to create an uproar in the assembly; a racket has been created, but little fruit! Whoever wants fruit must strain himself to change the feelings and force a surge of the compunction of the heart, true and deep…. Go to return a being taken by passion! It takes the hand of God. Also, the preacher must preach with his knees more than with his words (SSL, p. 325).

During missions, preaching about prayer was a new thing. It was he who introduced it into the list of sermons. He kept it there. There was no mission without a sermon on prayer, and if only one sermon could be given, the sermon on prayer must be given. But what prayer should be preached?—a prayer in the colors of the Gospel. Alphonsus's preaching was so convincing that the churches in the Redemptorist missionary communities soon became true schools for prayer. The little people of the countryside could say, each morning: "Let us go and pray with the Fathers!" "Pray"—the plan was exact. For Alphonsus, who said his rosary every day, did not invite them to recite the rosary, but to "pray"

with the Gospel. He taught the poor who, for the most part, were
illiterate, to "pray," beginning with the Word of God. To do that,
he invited the people, who did not know how to read, to gather,
for prayer as a family or at church. It was enough that one person
in the group knew how to read the texts that Alphonsus had written and published in their own language, so that all could take
advantage. For everyone understood this very simple language:

> My Jesus, my hope and my love, you were willing to lose
> your life so I would not be lost. I love you above every-
> thing, my Redeemer and my God.
>
> You gave yourself to me completely; I give you all my
> will, and with it, I repeat over and over that I love you;
> and I wish to keep on saying that I love you. And hear
> you always reply the same. That is what I always want to
> say in this life and that is how I want to die, breathing my
> last with these dear words on my lips: My God, I love
> you. May that be the beginning of an eternity of love, of
> a consecrated eternity, with no stopping and no end, lov-
> ing you.
>
> Yes, my Jesus, because I love you, I regret more than
> anything else that I have offended you…. This thought
> torments me more than any punishment, but it consoles
> me to think that I am dealing with infinite goodness, who
> will not despise a truly loving heart. My wish is that I
> could die for you, you who died for me!
>
> My dear Redeemer, I surely hope for eternal salvation
> in the life to come; in this life, I hope for holy persever-
> ance in your love; and, therefore, I intend to keep asking
> for it of you. Through the merits of your death, give me
> perseverance in praying to you. This, too, I ask and hope
> of you, O Mary, my Queen! (AA, pp. 30–1).

Saint Alphonsus, the Doctor of Prayer, prayed a great deal and
preached a great deal about prayer. He also wrote about this theme,
for he discovered the pastoral impact of the Christian press. That

was the origin of his two books on prayer. First, a small booklet of about twenty pages, which appeared in 1757: *A Short Treatise on the Necessity of Prayer*, which he concluded by announcing his second book on the subject:

> I hope to clearly demonstrate in it that the grace of prayer is given to everyone, in such a way that, if someone comes to damn himself, he has no excuse. In effect, God, universally grants everyone the grace of prayer continuously, without which there is no need for any other special help, and, by this prayer, receive the greatest help to vanquish all temptation and practice all virtues. But I cannot end this without showing the great sorrow that I experience when I see that amongst the preachers and confessors, there can be found only a few who speak of it; and if they speak of it, they speak too little, just in passing. For me, by seeing the necessity of prayer, I say that all spiritual books to their readers, all preachers to their listeners, all confessors to their penitents, in all preaching, in all confessions, must instill no other lesson insistently than to pray always. They must always have this exhortation on their lips, this warning: "pray, pray, pray, never abandon prayer...."

Two years later, in Naples, the second book that was promised appeared: *Prayer, the Great Means of Salvation*. In the introduction, we can read the following:

> I have written many different works on spirituality, but I estimate that I have never written anything more useful than this small booklet where I speak about prayer, the indispensable and sure way to obtain eternal salvation and all the graces we need. I don't have the possibility, but if I could, I would like to print as many copies of this book as there are faithful people living on the earth and distribute them to each person so that everyone would

understand the necessity for all of us to pray for our salvation.... Without prayer, according to ordinary providence, all of our meditations would remain useless, as
well as all of our resolutions and promises. If we do not
pray, we will always be unfaithful to all of the lights received from God and all of the commitments undertaken
(pp. 9–10 of the Lupi translation).

Pray because we love the Lord, pray to always love more, that is
the conviction that Alphonsus, the missionary, tried to instill in
everyone through his example, his words, and his writings. His
spirituality of prayer relies upon "the" prayer and not on "many"
forms of prayer. God is love; therefore, God will not refuse to
save us if we are sincere. One of his favorite thoughts has gone to
all corners of the globe: "Whoever prays, saves himself; whoever
does not pray, is lost. All of the saints were saved and sanctified
through prayer."

And then there is Mary: Alphonsus reminds us that "her
prayers are mother's prayers."

AND US, TODAY?

What is the quality of our contact with God in terms of prayer?
Are we not preoccupied with reciting one particular form or another of prayer (the rosary, litany, and so on)? Or do we want to
pray truly, that is, make contact with God, converse with him
like friends, or like a child with his parents? In short, do we truly
pray or how do we pray? Is our prayer primarily the recital of a
formal one, or a friendly meeting with God?

God speaks to our heart...on the condition that we take the
time to recognize him, the time to listen to him, to see him and to
let ourselves be seen by him, loved by him, and changed by him.
Where are we in this listening of the Word of God that is the
beginning of prayer?

And then, let us take the time to admire, to marvel at what
God does today within us and around us.

God alone is able to help us develop what is the best within each of us, and, with us, what is the best in others. Where are we with reference to this prayer: "may your will be done"? Finally, do we take the time to ask the Lord for his Holy Spirit? With the Holy Spirit, everything is the voice of God. Everything cries out his love. As Saint Alphonsus wrote in *On Conversing Continually and Familiarly With God* (pp. 33–7):

When you think about the rich countryside,
pleasant shores, flowers, and fruit that charm you
by their beauty and perfume, say:
"How many beautiful things
God has made for me here on earth!
Must I not love him?
And what other delights has he reserved
for me in heaven?"
In a vista of smiling hills and beautiful landscapes,
Saint Teresa reproached herself
for her ingratitude towards God.
The Abbey of Rancé, the founder of the Trappists,
found, in the beauties of nature,
an obligatory call to love God.
Penetrated with the same thoughts,
Saint Augustine said:
"The sky, the earth, and all the creatures preach to me,
Lord, of your love...."
A river, a simple brook, where the waters run to
the sea with no obstruction,
will remind you that your soul must always extend
towards God, your unique love....
By seeing a little dog who,
for a miserable piece of bread,
is so faithful to his master, ask yourself how much
more faithful you should be to this God
who has created you, keeps you alive,
extends providence over you and

fulfills you with so many benefits!
Do you hear the birds singing?
"My soul, listen how these creatures sing
praises to their Creator: and you?"
Then make yourself sing his praises through acts of love.
But if it's the rooster's song that resounds,
remember that, at another time,
you have denied your God like Saint Peter and then
renew your regrets and your tears....
To the appearance of the valleys,
consider that they are fertilized by the water that
descends from the mountains:
in the same way, the graces of heaven descend onto the
humble and leave the arrogant aside....
When your gaze stops on the sea,
reflect about the grandeur and immensity of God....
Multiply also, as much as possible,
the acts of love towards God.
It is there that we find, as Saint Teresa said,
"the wood that feeds the furnace of the holy love
in our heart"? Amen.

REFLECTION QUESTIONS

Is there a "spirituality of prayer" in my life? Do I pray using different methods, or not? Have I considered new methods of prayer for the sake of revitalizing my spiritual life? Perhaps consulting a priest, sister, or spiritual director would provide me with new ways to pray. Are my prayers often memorized and recited? If I no longer find this method of prayer helpful, might I consider a more conversational approach, an approach that speaks "from the heart"?

DAY THIRTEEN

One Hour and Four Ducats Lost!

FOCUS POINT

As a bishop, Alphonsus had many responsibilities within his diocese. We too bear many responsibilities to God in service and love as Christians. As Alphonsus was a "bishop of the present," so are we all "Christians of the present moment." We are to take immediate action whenever we see another person in need, because we see Jesus Christ in that person calling out for our love, attention, and service.

In the correspondence that was exchanged between Alphonsus and his printer, Remondini, in Venice, there were occasionally allusions to his health. We can notice a few (see SSL, p. 473): "I am old and my head betrays me. Also, from one day to the next, I wait for death" (June 4, 1761). "Almost every year, I get a serious illness. From one day to the next, I wait for death" (July 13, 1761).

Yet, what happened was not death at all, but his nomination

as bishop of Sant'Agata-dei-Goti! Saint Alphonsus was in a stupor! He had previously refused the bishopric of Palermo. Someone then suggested to him: "But you could refuse!" On the spot, Alphonsus wrote a letter of renunciation and refusal of the episcopate and handed it back to the messenger for the nunciature, with a sizeable tip: "See," he said in conclusion, "for this nonsense, I only lost an hour and four ducats. I wouldn't trade the congregation for all the kingdoms in the world!"

But Clement XIII remained firm on his order. Alphonsus buckled...he would be the bishop: a poor bishop, in a poor diocese; a bishop who was the friend of the poor. During his episcopal coronation, in July 1762, his secretary had a sumptuous meal prepared that did not please the bishop: "Don Felice, may God forgive you! What have you done! There are so many poor people who are dying of hunger and you want us to have a banquet!"

A straw mattress for the Monsignor, and the cap of a jug for his episcopal ring! The bishop was open to the poor people. Everyone could come visit him without making an appointment. "Our bishop is a saint.... We have a living saint!" said the people.

A true saint, in fact, and a missionary saint who cared for the most abandoned, the miserable, the poor, and the sinners. He preached everywhere, convinced that the primary role of a bishop was not to preside but to preach the Gospel and have it preached: "The greatest good that a bishop could gain for his diocese is to have missions preached every three years without fail. I will only ask you to pay attention to one thing from the time of the arrival of the missionaries: you must beg them to preach the missions in all of the villages, no matter how small they are. The purpose of the congregation is to preach the mission in a central location where they hope to unite all of the surrounding hamlets. False hope! A few pious persons came; but the sinful people, consequently the most in need, didn't go.... For me, in my diocese, I have the missions preached in all of the villages, even if they only have two hundred souls" (SSL, p. 532).

As a bishop, Alphonsus was very conscious of his responsibilities: he said "that his miter weighed very heavily on his conscience" (SSL, p. 374). Furthermore, "here, we must reveal one of the major characteristics of Alphonsus's mentality and conscience: responsibility is...for the people who are responsible. If, in the missions, he invites notable people to a particular retreat, it is not to flatter their social class, it is because of the weight that their decisions, spirit, and, above all, their example represents.

He vigorously insists on the responsibilities of each person at each level: in the diocese, 'the bishops depend upon the sanctification of the people'; in the parishes, 'the curates depend upon the progress or the loss of the faithful'; in the monasteries, 'all of the abuses are to be attributed to the priors and the confessors.' With respect to the seminaries, there must first be, not good seminarians, but 'a good rector,' 'good teachers,' and 'mature spiritual prefects' on hand" (SSL, p. 374).

Alphonsus was conscious of his responsibilities with respect to his diocese, but also with respect to the entire Church. Like the first apostles, he was anxious for all the churches (see 2 Cor 11:28). Pope Clement XIII, who obligated him to accept the bishopric, congratulated Alphonsus in a letter dated August 4, 1767, in response to the dedication of his book, *The Truth of the Faith*:

> We love you a great deal, venerable brother, because you are not content to just govern your Church: by letting nothing make you lose the time you have left, you dedicate it to work whose usefulness is not limited only to your diocese, but extends to the universal Church (SSL, p. 536).

To govern is to look ahead: thus, Alphonsus was a bishop of the future. Having just started his duties, he was preoccupied with expanding the seminary in the broadest sense, renewing the teaching staff, and promoting a better method for the selection of candidates. He shared his concern for the quality of vocations, for their accompaniment and training with the entire episcopate in a small book, *Reflections Useful for Bishops*, published in 1745:

The seminary trains good priests; and good priests are responsible for the spiritual good of all people. An orderly seminary will assure the sanctification of the diocese; if not, it will ruin it (SSL, p. 504).

A bishop of the future, Alphonsus Liguori was the bishop of vocations. One day, after one of his sermons, fifteen young men asked to consecrate themselves to God. Even if they were enthusiastic, Alphonsus considered his choices seriously. To one person, who had, for a long time, recommended a young man who proved to be clearly inapt for the priesthood, Alphonsus firmly stated: "Do you have anything else to say to me? No, well then take it as if you have spoken to a dead person!"

A bishop of the future, Alphonsus, however, was a bishop of the present, which included concrete actions on a daily basis. During the famine of 1764, he, himself, organized humanitarian aid for his diocese. He told his people: "Give, so that each will come back contented. They are only asking for what rightfully belongs to them." Had he not written in his *Reflections Useful for Bishops*:

> "For the bishop to understand well: the Church doesn't give him an allotment of money to be used foolishly; but to aid the poor"; and in his practical directives: "In cases of extreme necessity, the goods belong to everyone.... It is then the right of the poor to take from the rich" (SSL, p. 513).

Saint Alphonsus's spirituality is, then, a spirituality of a free man, a responsible adult. Grateful for the talents that the Master had entrusted to him, he took care of them in order to increase them. A pastor for people for whom he felt responsible, he helped them to blossom in the sunlight of the Gospel.

AND US, TODAY?

Are we concerned with increasing the gifts we have received? Are we conscious of our responsibilities? In this vein, have we chosen to devote ourselves to a certain activity in the Church, or have we chosen Jesus Christ as if he were a lover?

Does our choice of Christ lead us to always work more in the Church, in the spirit of Vatican Council II, that is, as "a Church which serves the poor"?

Furthermore, where are we with respect to our collaboration with the charitable and humanitarian actions of the Church and of the society in which we live?

And then, have we, like the first apostles, like Paul, like Alphonsus, "concern for all churches"?

Where are we in our preparation for the future? What is our participation in the new evangelization of the world to which Pope John Paul II has called us?

Finally, are we concerned with vocations, all vocations, including the priesthood, deacons, and religious in our local churches? Do we pray for the vocations? And, above all, to be more faithful to our own vocations so that, always and everywhere, the will of the love of the Father will triumph?

> *What is the great goal of those souls*
> *who truly love God?*
> *It is to conform themselves,*
> *at all times, to his divine will.*
> *And this is what Jesus taught us to pray for,*
> *that we may be able to fulfill the will of God here on earth,*
> *with as much perfection as the blessed do in heaven:*
> *"...thy will be done here on earth as it is in heaven."*
> *Saint Teresa made an offering of her will to God at*
> *least fifty times every day; and like David, who said:*
> *"My heart is steadfast,*
> *O God, my heart is steadfast" (Ps 57:7).*
> *Ah, admire the power of one perfect act of conformity*
> *to the will of God;*

it changes a sinner into a saint,
as happened to Saint Paul, who,
by following God's instructions about what
he should do (see Acts 9:6), changed from a persecutor
of the Church into an apostle and vessel of election....
O my God, I have not acted in this way!
How often I have followed my own will
and scorned yours.
But then I didn't love you,
but now I love you more than myself.
I embrace all of your divine decisions;
I want to please you in everything.
You know my weakness, give me the strength
to keep my resolution.
O Mary, obtain the grace for me to always do the
will of God for the remainder of my life.
Amen (VS, pp. 168–9).

REFLECTION QUESTIONS

Being a Christian, what specific responsibilities do I recognize as mine? Do I feel a pull to serve the poor, feed the hungry, or pray for an increase in vocations to the priesthood and religious life? What specific organizations available in my parish or community might I consider joining so I can address this responsibility to serve God by serving those in need?

DAY FOURTEEN

Here I Am, My God

FOCUS POINT

Saint Alphonsus gave his entire life to God. Every day, every minute, every moment of Alphonsus's life was given over to God. He thought of God at every moment, and we are called to do the same, until the hour of our death. We must seek to live in the present moment with God, to devote every part of our person, every second of our day to his presence. This is the holiness Saint Alphonsus sought in his own life.

Monsignor Liguori would be the bishop of Sant'Agata-dei-Goti until 1775. When the pope accepted his resignation, someone teased him and commented: "You seem to have straightened yourself up." The Monsignor replied: "I have lifted the weight of Mount Taburno off my shoulders!" (Note: Mount Taburno was the mountain that dominated the small diocese.) Released from the episcopate, Alphonsus continued his mission: he wrote, he welcomed, he prayed. He worked to the very limits of his strength. Then, when he stopped publishing, he left us 111 works. Many are pocket books of popular piety, but the most important are the thick volumes of his *Moral Theology*. Yet, what characterizes this colossal work is that it is not organized like a course on Christian doctrine. Alphonsus was not a teacher, he was an educator. For him, as for the Fathers of the Church, the Bible was not primarily a series of laws, it was primarily a means of education. His entire work proposes a development of the Christian personality that could satisfy the highest aspirations of the humanism of the Century of Enlightenment. Thus, it unites with the preoccupation of the Greek Fathers, such as Clement of Alexandria or Gregory of Nyssa, who knew to invent a Christian pedagogy that was built from the resources of the Greek one. Alphonsus didn't waste his time, writing in his book, *The Way of Salvation*:

> Nothing is as precious as time, and yet why is it valued so little? Some people will spend hours joking or standing around, wasting the better part of a day, looking out of a window or standing outside to see what everyone else is doing, and, if you ask them what they are doing, they will tell you that they are passing time. O how despised time now is! It will be wanted all the more by these people when death surprises them....
>
> The time of death is the time of night, when nothing can be seen or accomplished.... Hence, the Holy Spirit admonishes us to walk in the way of the Lord, while we still have the light to do it....
>
> Who knows, maybe the meditation I am now reading may be the last I shall ever cast my eyes on? (VS, pp. 54–5).

And Alphonsus continued his mission right up until the very end. In 1781, he knew the supreme trial for a founder: his young congregation was cut in half by a pontifical decision. In effect, following difficult negotiations with the aim to obtain the approval of the king of Naples, negotiations that Alphonsus could not lead himself, Pius VI took advantage of that occasion to settle his differences with the "regalness" of Fernand IV (the king of Naples). He refused to recognize the royal *claim* and only recognized the missions which were located in the pontifical states. Later, after the death of Alphonsus, Pius VI would declare: "He was a saint! I tortured a saint!" But, for the moment, Alphonsus was heartbroken over it. However, he never stopped saying: "All I need is God, he is enough for me, I only need his grace. The pope wants it his way: Blessed is God!"

Alphonsus was approaching his death: he celebrated Mass for the last time on November 25, 1785: "Jesus Christ no longer wants me to celebrate. May his will be done." He often asked, as he became even more avid, for the Eucharist: "Give me Jesus Christ." And he spent complete half-days before the tabernacle. We can easily imagine him repeating the prayer that he wrote on the first pages of his *Visits to the Blessed Sacrament*:

> *O Jesus, my Sovereign Master, your love for mankind*
> *keeps you in this Majestic Sacrament night and day....*
> *I believe in your presence in the holy Eucharist.*
> *I adore you from the abyss of my nothingness;*
> *I thank you for all of the graces you have bestowed*
> *upon me and, in particular,*
> *for having given me yourself in the Eucharist and for*
> *having given me your most holy Mother,*
> *Mary, as my advocate, and for having called me to visit*
> *you in this church.*
> *Today, I come to pay homage to your all-loving heart....*
> *My Jesus, I love you with all of my heart.*
> *I repent for having so often offended your infinite*
> *goodness in the past. I promise,*
> *with the help of your grace, to never offend you again;*
> *presently, as miserable and unworthy as I am,*
> *I consecrate myself to you completely;*
> *I give myself to you and completely renounce my will,*
> *my affections, and all of my desires; in a phrase,*

all that I have. From this time on, use me as you will.
All I ask of you is what I want above everything else:
your holy love, final perseverance, and the perfect
fulfillment of your will. Amen (VSS, pp. 123–4).

On July 16, 1787, an intense fever warned that the end was near.
In his rare moments of consciousness, he could be heard to say:
"Here I am, my God!" or "Come, my Jesus!" On July 30, "as we
presented a crucifix to him...he closed his hands around it with
love and made the effort to kiss it three times. The following day,
August 1...in the Lord, he died at the sound of the Angelus" (SSL,
pp. 625–6). Alphonsus had just lived his final apostolate: communion with the death and resurrection of Jesus. It was the final
gift of his life. Up until then, he had only given pieces of his long
life. In that last instant, he could give it all. Definitively. Death,
for Jesus on the cross, was the time of his greatest love. It was the
same for Alphonsus.

Jesus was waiting for him. His last meeting was written into
a long friendship. It was the meeting with the risen Lord, the
Easter sun who tears away the clouds here below...and invites
him to enter into the banquet room of the kingdom of heaven.

AND US, TODAY?

Are we conscious of the fact that the Christian faith needs to be
born into the culture of the modern world in order to exist? In
effect, isn't the Church in charge of the Good News for mankind?

Are we conscious of the importance for the Church to be able
to send an audible and credible evangelical message out through
the various media? That was Alphonsus's greatness in the eighteenth century, to have evangelized Europe with the resources of
only a burgeoning printing industry. And us?

Are we conscious of the importance of our "final apostolate"?
He doesn't improvise, he prepares himself...in the prayer to the
Lord and our Lady. On this last stretch of road, our brothers and
sisters on earth can no longer follow us: we visit the sick, we

accompany the dying, certainly. But we take the last step alone. However, it can be done, hand in hand, with the Lord, under the benevolent gaze of our Lady. For if Christ already connected us with his work of salvation throughout our active life, we can be even more connected to him at the hour of our death, when we will definitively be united in communion to this death and resurrection that will transform us, and work to transform the world, in him, through him, and with him. For our eternal happiness.

"Shout aloud and sing for joy, O royal Zion,
for great in your midst is the Holy One of Israel" (Isa 12:6).
What joy, hopes, and affections must fill our hearts at
the thought that in the midst of our land,
in our churches, close to us,
lives and dwells Jesus Christ,
the most Holy of Holies, the true God!
He whose presence makes the saints in heaven rejoice!
He who is love itself!
Here I am, Lord, I give myself completely to you:
I dedicate the remainder of my life, from now on,
to a love that is always more intense for
the most holy Sacrament.
Eucharistic Jesus, be my consolation and my only love
during my life and at my death....
Amen, amen. Such is my hope:
may I be worthy to realize it.
When, O my Jesus, shall I see the splendor of your
face? Amen (VSS, pp. 190–1).

REFLECTION QUESTIONS

Do I seek to make myself present to God at every moment of my day? Are there distractions in my life that keep me from giving myself totally over to God? What are these distractions? How can I address these obstacles (concerns for those things less than God, regrets for the past, anxieties for the future) in my prayer life?

The Blessed Virgin Tells Me So Many Beautiful Things

FOCUS POINT

Saint Alphonsus had a tremendous devotion to the Blessed Virgin Mary. We are also called to foster a devotion to the Mother of God. Mary is our great intercessor. From the wedding at Cana to the present day, Mary intercedes for all those who call out for her aid. Mary intercedes to God on our behalf, securing his graces for our benefit, and bringing those graces to us. We need only call out to her in prayer.

F ather G. B. Costanzo tell us: "The year before his death, I asked Alphonsus, after he had made his confession, if he had the desire to see the Blessed Virgin at the moment of death, and did he feel supported by her." Alphonsus answered:

Listen to me. When I was young, I often spoke with the Madonna. She counseled me about all of the affairs of the congregation. [She told me] so many things, so many beautiful things... (SSL, p. 286).

What is certain is that Alphonsus wrote many beautiful pages about the Madonna in his book, *The Glories of Mary*. This work, begun in 1734 in the community of Villa Liberi, would be the masterpiece of his heart. Alphonsus took sixteen years to complete it. This book would become a bestseller—"the greatest draw of all time: thousands of editions have been printed since 1750" (René Laurentin, *A Short Treatise on the Virgin Mary*).

"...this Immaculate Virgin in whom you have placed our hope and the assurance of our salvation, redeemed by your blood" (GM, p. xxi). This phrase, from Alphonsus, placed at the beginning of his book, in the prayer he addressed to his "most loving Redeemer and Lord Jesus Christ" (ibid), well sums up his Marian devotion. Yet, in the eighteenth century, singing *The Glories of Mary* would have caused an uproar: Alphonsus went against the current of a Christian world that was characterized by rationalism, Protestantism, and Jansenism. He knew that. That is why he took the time to give us a few explanations:

In the world, when we love a person, it is customary to speak of them and praise them so that these individuals will be esteemed and praised by others.... Those who really love our Lady...endeavor to praise her always and everywhere to make the whole world love her.... So that everyone may be convinced, both for our own good and for the good of the Christian people, how important it is to promote devotion to Mary (GM, pp. xxiii–xxiv).

The goal of this work is then clear: it is not a technical study of Mary in order to develop better theories about her. No, it is simply to help people—primarily the little people—to love Mary, and to pray to her with a fervor like that of the Gospel, the liturgy, and the tradition of the Fathers of the Church, just as Alphonsus was in the habit of doing himself, in his Marian preaching, each Saturday throughout his religious life:

> I leave it to other authors to praise the other prerogatives of Mary and I confine myself, for the most part, to her mercy and the power of her intercession. I have gathered, as far as I was able (and it was the work of many years), all that the Fathers of the Church and the most celebrated authors have to say on the subject. I find that the mercy and the power of our Lady are admirably portrayed in the prayer *Salve Regina* (Hail, Holy Mary)...which marvelously describes this power and mercy of the Virgin Mary, I have endeavored...to divide and explain this beautiful prayer, point by point (GM, p. xxv).

After each commentary of a verse of the *Salve Regina*, Alphonsus gives us a very simple prayer: often, we find traces of the former lawyer in them:

> *O sweet Virgin Mary, O tender Advocate,*
> *perform your task for me....*
> *Do not say that my case is too difficult to be won,*
> *for I know, and everybody tells me, that every case,*
> *no matter how desperate it may be,*
> *if undertaken by you, will never be lost.*
> *Will mine be lost? No, I have no fear of this.*
> *The only things I might be afraid of is that,*
> *on seeing the number of my sins,*
> *you might be disinclined to defend me.*
> *But, in view of your immense mercy and the great*
> *desire of your ever loving heart to help*
> *even the most abandoned sinners,*
> *I do not fear even this.*

Who ever was lost who appealed to you?
That is why I invoke your help.
O my great advocate, my refuge, my hope,
my Mother Mary (GM, p. 114).

This is a prayer of hope: we can breathe in the fervor of the young Christian, who, since his "conversion" in 1722, each evening went, after his visit to a church where the Blessed Sacrament was exposed, into another church in Naples dedicated to the Blessed Virgin:

O Mother of Mercy, since you are so merciful and so
eager to help us shortsighted creatures and
grant our prayers, I, the most miserable of all,
appeal to your mercy today
and beg you to grant what I ask.
Let others ask what they please: health of body,
earthly possessions, and advantages.
But I ask you, O Mary,
for the things that you desire me to ask for,
the things that are most in accordance with your will
and most pleasing to your holy heart.
You were so humble:
obtain for me humility and love for contempt.
You were so patient amid the trials of this life:
obtain for me patience in adversity.
You were so full of love for God:
obtain for me the gift of a pure and holy love.
You were all loving towards your neighbor:
obtain for me love for others,
above all for those who are against me.
You were so united to the will of God:
obtain for me complete conformity to the will of God
in whatever way he may be pleased to dispose of me.
Finally, you are the most holy of all creatures:
O Mary, make me a saint....

O Mary, my Mother, my Hope...Amen
(GM, pp. 148–9).

"Mary, my Hope"—this phrase is dear to Saint Alphonsus. He wrote it with his own hand under the lithograph of the Madonna that he designed for the frontispiece of the first edition of *The Glories of Mary*, his book, he, himself, said "about hope in Mary." This hope followed him throughout his life all the way to his last hours:

> The end was near.... On July 28 we gave him his engraving of our Lady, inspired by Carlo Dolci (1616–1686). He looked at it, his lips moving, and opened his arms in a gesture of offering.... On July 29, he said, "Give me the Madonna." He took it in his hands and prayed.... On July 31, around 6:00 P.M., while he was holding the image of the Blessed Virgin in his hands, all of a sudden we saw his face inflamed and become shining as he was speaking in a low voice and smiling at the Madonna (HSE, pp. 261–2).

Furthermore, in his book, *Prayers for Our Lady for Each Day of the Week* (1734), Alphonsus wrote:

> *Majestic Sovereign—pardon my boldness—come,*
> *before I take my last breath, come in person to console*
> *me with your presence.*
> *Without a doubt, I am only a sinner,*
> *I am not worthy of this favor;*
> *but I am your servant, I love you,*
> *and my trust in you is without limitations,*
> *O Mary! I then wait for you; don't disappoint my hope.*
> *Anyway,...at least help me from heaven so that I leave*
> *this life loving God and you, O my Mother, to then*
> *continue to love you eternally in paradise (VS, p. 384).*

The following day, August 1, Alphonsus died in peace when the Pagani bells chimed the noon Angelus. He was holding the Madonna in his hands. His prayer reached its completion on the threshold of the Father's house. It was finally the awaited meeting, the savory fruit of this hope that was lifted from all of his prayers, especially his Marian prayer (from *Consideration on the Religious Vocation*, volume 11, p. 299):

O my Sovereign, if you pray for me, I will be saved,
for you obtain all that you want from your divine Son.
Pray then for me, majestic Mother of God,
so that your Son will hear you and grant your wishes.
It is true that I am not worthy of your protection,
but you have never abandoned anyone
who has had recourse to you.
O Mary, I consecrate my soul to you:
it is up to you to save it. Obtain for me perseverance
through divine grace and love for your Son
and for you.
I love you, O my Queen,
and I hope to love you forever.
Love me, keep me under the mantle of your protection,
and have pity on me, I ask you through the love that
you bring to your beloved Jesus.
Consider how much trust I have in your mercy...
I know it well, you will always help me,
so much that I will faithfully pray to you:
that is another grace you must obtain for me each time
that temptation puts me in danger of losing God.
Help me, above all, at the hour of my death;
make it so that I breathe my last breath by uttering
your name, and that of your divine Son,
by saying to you: Jesus and Mary,
I commend my soul to you.

Let us repeat it again: the secret of Alphonsus's spirituality rests in his two loves—Jesus and Mary. But this burning and radiant love, which he never stopped sharing with the Christian people through his works, words, and his example, was always colored with hope, as we can see in the following, one of the first of his poems:

> *Do you know my desire,*
> *O tender Mary?*
> *You, my Hope,*
> *I would like to love you,*
> *Keep me always at your side;*
> *Most beautiful queen,*
> *Don't chase me away.*
> *When it is your turn, tell me,*
> *Rose of my heart,*
> *O Mother of love:*
> *What do you want from me?*
> *I know nothing to offer you*
> *Other than my own heart;*
> *From a loving hand,*
> *I make a gift of it to you (SSL, p. 77).*

AND US, TODAY?

Is our spirituality a Marian spirituality? Is it always colored with hope?

What place do we give to Mary in our Christian life? Have we finally understood that God, himself, wanted us to be a member of the divine family, and that Mary holds a special choice place, that the communion of saints must always enlighten our prayer and action even more? Mary is not a saint like the others, she is not a goddess, certainly, but the mother of Jesus. She is the responsible woman who said "yes" in our name on the day of the Annunciation, and who labored painfully, at the foot of the cross, giving birth to the Church, in communion with her crucified son. Furthermore, is she not the Immaculate One, the new Eve, the most perfect human creature, the one, who, in her Assumption, fully reunites with her son in his paschal mystery? The One who precedes us to heaven, by communing like no other person in the world, to the mystery of love of the death and resurrection of her son, Jesus?

That was the merit of Saint Alphonsus, the great lawyer of Naples, to take on Mary's defense in the middle of the eighteenth century when faced with Jansenists and all those who were cold and scorned Marian devotion. Today, he still invites us to leave a religion that would simply be just a lovely theory about God, even less a powerful religious organization, to enter, with confidence, into the holy "family" of the Lord. Mary, the mother of Jesus, occupies a special place there which she uses to help her children, especially those who ask for her intercession in faithfulness to the traditions of the Christian people:

O holy and Immaculate Virgin!
O creature most exalted and most humble!
You were so lowly in your own eyes,
but so great in the eyes of the Lord that he exalted you
and chose you for his Mother,
and then made you queen of heaven and earth.
I thank God therefore for having honored you so
greatly, and I rejoice in seeing you so closely united to
him that no other creature can ever be your equal....
Hail Mary, full of grace.
You are already full of grace;
grant a portion of that grace to me.
The Lord is with you. That Lord who was always
with you from the very first moment of your creation
has now united himself more closely to you by
becoming your Son.
Blessed are you among women. O Mary, blessed
among all women, obtain divine blessing for us also.
And blessed is the fruit of thy womb, Jesus.

O blessed plant which has given the world such a
noble and holy fruit!
Holy Mary, Mother of God. O Mary,
I acknowledge that you are the true Mother of God,
and to defend this truth,
I am willing to lay down my life a thousand times.
Pray for us sinners. Even though you are the
Mother of God, you are also the Mother of our
salvation and of us poor sinners.
God became man to save sinners,
and made you his Mother so that your prayers might
be powerful enough to save any sinner.
Hasten then, O Mary, and pray for us, now,
and at the hour of our death. Pray always!
Pray now when we live in the midst of so many
temptations and dangers of losing God;
but still more, pray for us at the hour of our death,
when we are about to leave this world and appear
before God's tribunal;
so that, being saved by the merits of Jesus Christ and
by your intercession, we may come one day without
fear of being lost to greet and praise you with your Son
in heaven for all eternity. Amen (GM, pp. 232–3).

REFLECTION QUESTIONS

In what ways do I seek to foster my devotion to the Blessed Virgin? Do I make praying the rosary a regular part of my spiritual life? Might consulting a priest, sister, or spiritual director aid me in fostering a stronger devotion to Mary, and through that help my understanding of my part in the holy "family" of the Lord, and my part in the Church as a whole?

Prayer to Saint Alphonsus Liguori

Brother Alphonsus, our blessed father,
permit your faithful companions and friends
to open their hearts to you.
See what we are.
We know who you were and what you have done.
We let ourselves be moved by your face and by the
indications of your passage.
We scrutinize your story and your spirituality
so as to better grasp your fundamental intuitions
and your message,
but we run the risk of forgetting that you are alive,
today, close to the Father and close to us.

You are our Brother.
Also, consider as if it is truly your own the spiritual
family who has recourse to you.
See how bloodstained and fragile it is today.
With us, count those who have left and the small
number of those remaining.
With us, count the number of our brothers and sisters
who are sick or advanced in age.
Look at all of those who have been too shaken by the
stormy trials of life and whose hope is weakened.
Consider the troubled and agitated world
into which we are plunged.

Your time, or at least what we know of it,
is not the same as ours. Our God, our Christ,
our faith—certainly they have not changed—but man,
the culture, and society have been so upset.
We are bombarded with new questions and
often find ourselves lacking answers.
Can you measure how weak we are, how anxious,
and the doubts that bombard us?

Brother Alphonsus, our blessed father,
you wanted your spiritual sons and daughters to
dedicate themselves to the proclamation
of the Good News to the poor
and marginal people of society.
You, yourself, gave us a good example with your work
with those who were excluded by life:
those condemned to death in prisons, and those who
had incurable illnesses in the hospitals of Naples;
those who society excludes: the lazzaroni and the poor
of the worst neighborhoods; those excluded by the
Church: the little people of the hamlets, abandoned in
the countryside; those excluded from eternal salvation:
men and women broken by an impractical morality;
those excluded by knowledge:
the countless illiterate who composed ninety-five
percent of the population at that time.
In the footsteps of the Master and the apostles, you
walked to seek the "lost sheep."
You went to meet them through your writings as well
as through your words and the testimony of your life.

At a time when everything is a problem,
may we proclaim the Gospel with enthusiasm and keep
us from letting it fade.
And then, remember the time when you dreamed of
leaving for far-off missions.

In our hearts, keep alive the taste for new horizons,
the missionary emergencies, and the
"new worlds" to evangelize.
Brother Alphonsus, you see it, our present is difficult,
our future is uncertain. Awaken our hope.
Provoke our courage. Help our ardor.
Reveal the truth of our task to us.
We await your help and support;
you who are close to the heart of God,
intercede for the family that you have founded.
With our Lady, persevere in the prayer for your sons
and daughters. May the Holy Spirit of the Pentecost,
whose fire inflames you, descend upon us all.
May our efforts and sorrows multiply,
in a way that pleases the Lord.
May the tenacity of some and the talents of others
bring fruit for the glory of the risen Christ.

Finally, Brother Alphonsus, our father,
we thank you for this path that
you have opened before us, for your loving presence
and the prayer with which you surround us.
You are with us.
May we, with you, "continue Christ today." Amen.

Bibliography

Jones, CSsR, Frederick M. *Alphonsus de Liguori: Saint of Bourbon Naples, 1696–1787, and Founder of the Redemptorists.* Liguori Publications, 1992.

Liguori, Saint Alphonsus. *The Glories of Mary.* Liguori Publications, 2000.

———. *Meditation for Lent.* Edited by Thomas M. Santa, CSsR. Liguori Publications, 1999.

———. *Meditations on the Eucharist.* Edited by Thomas M. Santa, CSsR. Liguori Publications, 1997.

———. *The Practice of the Love of Jesus Christ.* Translated by Peter Heinegg. Liguori Publications, 1997.

———. *Preparation for Death: Prayers and Consolations for the Final Journey.* Edited by Norman Muckerman, CSsR. Liguori Publications, 1998.

———. *Selected Writings and Prayers of Saint Alphonsus.* Adapted for modern readers by John Steingraeber, CSsR. Liguori Publications, 1997.

———. *Visits to the Most Blessed Sacrament and the Blessed Virgin Mary.* Liguori Publications, 1994.

———. *The Way of Saint Alphonsus Liguori: Selected Writings on the Spiritual Life.* Compiled with an introduction by Barry Ulanov, Ph.D. Liguori Publications, 1999.

———. *Way of the Cross.* Revised by Thomas M. Santa, CSsR. Liguori Publications. 1999.

Londoño B., CSsR, Noel, general editor. *To Be a Redemptorist Today: Reflections on the Redemptorist Charism.* Liguori Publications, 1996.

Moran, CSsR, Terrence J. *In the Spirit of Saint Alphonsus: 30 Prayer Services for the Church Year with 6 in Spanish.* Liguori Publications, 2000.

Rey-Mermet, CSsR, Théodule. *Moral Choices: The Moral Theology of Saint Alphonsus Liguori.* Translated by Paul Laverdure. Liguori Publications, 1998.

———. *Saint Alphonsus Liguori: Tireless Worker for the Most Abandoned.* Translated from the second French edition by Jehanne-Marie Marchesi. New City Press, 1989.

Swanston, Hamish F. G. *Celebrating Eternity Now: A Study in the Theology of Saint Alphonsus de Liguori.* Liguori Publications, 1995.